The NEW
PASSPORT

MW01030159

12 Steps To Self-Sufficient Living

by Rita Bingham *and* Esther Dickey

Foreword by James Talmage Stevens, author of the best-selling **Making the Best of Basics—Family Preparedness Handbook** and **Don't Get Caught With *Your* Pantry Down!**

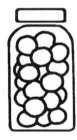

The New Passport To Survival is your Passport To Peace, your ticket to a self-sufficient lifestyle - whether you choose to live in a city, a suburb, or in a rural area. This book will show you how to prepare, without panicking, for all kinds of disasters—loss of a job, natural and man-made disasters, or global calamities.

NATURAL MEALS PUBLISHING
Edmond, Oklahoma

ISBN 1-882314-24-7
$15.95

Published by Natural Meals Publishing, Edmond, Oklahoma.
Website: www. naturalmeals.com
E-mail: info@naturalmeals.com
OR sales@naturalmeals.com
Phone/Fax: 405.359.3492
Order Line: 888.232.6706

Printed in the United States of America

Cover design by Rita Bingham
Illustrations by Clair Bingham

For:

My mother, Esther Dickey, who at 83 still exemplifies cheerfulness, courage, health and vitality. She has spent her lifetime serving others, beautifying her home and gardens, and working hard at living her motto "Use it up. Wear it out. Make it DO!...or do without." Thanks, Mom, for the great work you did in writing the original Passport and for the heritage of "stick-to-it-iveness" you passed on to your children.

Esther, and other courageous women like her, refuse to get caught up in the scurry and flurry of unimportant things that pull us away from home and family, from nurturing and nourishing, creating, beautifying, spreading peace and happiness, and preparing for an ever more uncertain future.

Special Thanks to:

My wonderful husband, Clair, for his artwork to help bring a little humor into an otherwise humorless topic - preparedness. His wise counsel and attention to detail have been invaluable in our own 30+ years of preparing for the unexpected. Together we have weathered many financial disasters and disappointments. Because of our commitment to store food, equipment and other supplies, we have never suffered or been fearful of where to find our next meal. We have enjoyed living by a family motto: "Be Prepared—And Fear Not."

Foreword

It is a personal joy for me to be a part of history repeating itself! The original **Passport To Survival,** authored by Esther Dickey, was the work of an inspired professional. She charted the path for a simpler and healthier lifestyle on an emergency diet by utilizing four basic foods—wheat, powdered milk, honey, and salt. Esther's wisdom and practicality have been recognized for many years. I certainly consider her the matron saint of food storage!

Rita Bingham, by updating her mother's work, is continuing to provide guidance and skills for a simpler lifestyle. In fact, she's known as the **"Bean Queen,"** principally because of her expertise and publications on how to cook dry beans in only 3 minutes. She has created nutritious recipes for every meal of the day using whole grains and legumes—great-tasting dishes even children enjoy. Now Rita is expanding her influence in the food storage and preparedness industry by revising and updating the information found in the original **Passport** in this new book, **The New Passport To Survival.** This version will teach readers how to utilize *"...seven foods and more to use and store..."* expanding on what her mother taught before. This timely volume will help anyone who intends to be better prepared for the uncertain future.

I urge readers to do something positive about being prepared—everyone can do something more now than has been done in the past. We can always improve our state of readiness. It is always practical and prudent to be prepared to deal with that which we cannot control. There is wisdom here—make it your wake-up call to be ahead of coming changes which could affect your life and the lives of your loved ones.

Rita has a great heritage. Readers will appreciate her efforts to make this information available so they can be better able to deal with future events. Remember this: *"There are no emergencies for those who are truly prepared."*

James Talmage Stevens, Author

Making the Best of Basics—Family Preparedness Handbook
Don't Get Caught With Your Pantry Down!

About the Author

Since 1966, Rita Bingham has taught and encouraged healthy eating. She carries on the tradition of her mother, Esther Dickey, who over 30 years ago wrote the original **Passport to Survival**, and Skills for Survival (a self-sufficiency manual of basic skills for surviving major and minor disasters).

Continuing in the tradition of her preparedness-oriented family, Rita uses wholesome, basic foods and imaginative techniques to create fast, high fiber recipes for every meal of the day, even snacks and desserts! Her husband and 5 children, as well as thousands of seminar participants, have given Rita's recipes rave reviews.

Rita has written and self-published three cookbooks and one guidebook on healthful eating; produced a training video to demonstrate some of the many ways nutritious foods can be prepared in a minimum amount of time; written articles for newspapers and magazines; and co-hosted a radio show providing information and recipes for healthy eating. She has consulted for companies to help answer their food questions and create marketable products. Rita has also provided training on how to include nutritious foods in weight loss programs.

Many seminar participants and customers ask if Rita and her family REALLY eat the healthy meals found in her books or if she just enjoys making up recipes and writing books. The answer is YES...the family really does eat this type of food. While they've all strayed at times from the high-fiber "back to basics" foods to eating "normal" foods (the white, the sugary and the fatty ones), they admit that good food makes them FEEL good and greatly improves health (making a visit to the doctor a *very* rare occasion), as well as keeping weight normal. When the children were small, they loved to learn about the nutrients in foods.

Rita enjoys finding ways to make more nutritious meals in less time. Experimenting in the kitchen has been a lifelong hobby for her, and she enjoys finding creative ways of sneaking healthy foods into traditional recipes.

More and more people are becoming increasingly aware of how good foods help them feel better physically, mentally and emotionally. The *Natural* **Meals In Minutes** style of eating is designed for those who recognize the importance of taking responsibility for their health and well being. Does this way of eating take more time than opening a can or a box? Certainly, but your health is worth it! ❤

Preface

32 years ago, in the original Passport To Survival, my mother wrote these statements, to which I have added some of my own words:

I believe that America is a nation with a prophetic mission to fulfill. Its discovery, colonization, revolution and constitutional structure were all under the influence of divine guidance. It was designed to be a great and free nation. Its history has been a reflection of its role as a beacon light to the world, a refuge and a promised land, a Christian nation. It was intended never to be destroyed, so long as its people would obey God's commandments.

Unfortunately, every nation seems to be getting progressively more disobedient to the will of God. Many scriptural references indicate that the downward spiral, both morally and spiritually, will continue until a new day dawns with the second coming of Jesus Christ, the "Prince of Peace." The evil influences that are abroad in the world today, filling men's hearts with discord and contention, will at that time be eradicated. With the coming of the "Brighter Day," wars will end and peace and happiness will exist for all of God's children who remain on earth.

Throughout the time leading up to this event, our mental and physical well-being will depend on how well we are prepared and how well we are conditioned to accept changes in times of chaos. Our standard of living will be in proportion to the preparation we have made to be independent and to provide for our own and our family's daily necessities. A big factor in it all will be our mental and spiritual outlook, our faith and our courage.

Faith In God Is the Key

Faith is not an abstract principle, but an inspiration for living. It elevates the spirit, giving zest and vigor to daily life and imparting enthusiastic assurance for the future. I choose to meet and end each day on my knees, giving thanks for God's great gifts and blessings and seeking His guidance.

Faith engenders hope which is part of the positive, optimistic way of life essential to true health and happiness. One who has this, and has made the necessary material preparations, can hope to survive any difficulties and calamities which may overtake the world. In the final analysis, what matters more than this?

Table Of Contents

PART ONE
WHY STORE?

CHAPTER 1

NIGHTMARE 2000

Over the years, there have been many predictions of possible "earth-shaking" events in the future. As I write this book, I see and hear daily reports of wars and rumors of war in the middle east; the economic crisis in Asian countries that is adversely affecting the world economy; companies downsizing; the lowest oil prices in 50 years (when you consider the value of the American dollar), causing massive layoffs in the industry; worldwide reports on the effects of El Niño—hurricanes, tornadoes and extreme weather conditions causing drought or flooding; "Y2K"- the problem of computer non-compliance at the beginning of the new century that could trigger financial chaos and cause global shortages, including food, water and power.

While there will certainly be repercussions from some or all of these events, no one can accurately predict the myriad of problems we will face, or how long into the 21st century we will be affected by the problems or panic caused by Y2K. Even the "experts" can't agree on whether this problem will turn out to be an inconvenience or a major catastrophe. Perhaps these depressing and calamitous events will not drastically change our daily lives, but there are other nightmare possibilities ahead, particularly in the field of food supply.

America's vast food surpluses have been drastically reduced. In his book **Many Are Called but Few Are Chosen,** Verlan Andersen sums it up in this way: "With less than ten percent of the population engaged in farming and with this small group almost completely dependent upon a continuing supply of fuel, machinery, and smoothly functioning transportation network, famine could and would stalk the land within a matter of weeks if anything interrupted the operation of this highly interdependent system of food production and distribution. Food markets would empty within hours and people would be left to their own devices to provide themselves with sustenance. The magnitude of the tragedy which could result is horrible to contemplate."

Strikes and other problems threaten the distribution of everything we buy; civil disorder and lawlessness menace our society; and nuclear weapons in the hands of ruthless leaders continue to be produced. Any or all of these factors could bring, at any time, a nightmare"2000"—a nightmare of famine and, for the unprepared, deprivation and even starvation.

To dramatize this situation, share with me this bad dream—a dream so vivid and real that you cannot get it off your mind. In the dream you are in a market with your basket and grocery list. A sick feeling comes over you as you look down the aisles and see row after row of grocery shelves almost empty. You have eight items on your shopping list, but only two are available, and these are the least essential. There is not even a loaf of bread in the store, nor any milk.

Having five children to feed, you are overcome with panic. You rush home and sit in the chair by the window—frustrated, bewildered,worn out. Looking across the street you see a whole family arriving at the Taylors. They are walking. The older boy is carrying the baby on his back, and everyone has big bundles—probably clothes and other portable necessities. Mrs. Taylor takes them all in the house.

In the way dreams have of mixing general impressions and specific detail, you get a feeling of overall confusion and uncertainty. The Paulsons, who have farmed their land in peace for fifty years, are besieged with people who trample over their fields stealing their cabbage and squash. Goods are being stolen from the stores, markets and schools are closed, many people are out of work. The car is out of gas and your husband rides your son's bicycle looking for work. You are told there are carrots and potatoes available further out in the country, and since there is almost no food in the house you decide to walk there. You search among all your shoes for sturdy oxfords to walk in but can't find any. You feel trapped, with your husband and the children home and not knowing from one meal to the next what to give them to eat.

Your mind flashes constantly to something new to worry about—like winter coming, a cold house with a silent furnace because you have no money to pay the utility bill, the wood supply for the fireplace almost depleted. You worry about the children getting sick and what you'd do if you couldn't get an appointment with the doctor, who is working to the breaking point already with all the sickness in town.

Depressing visions of Thanksgiving day and Christmas flood your mind. The children are fretting and unhappy because the family can't spend either of these occasions with their grandparents. You think of past Thanksgiving and Christmas holidays when happy times and delicious dinners were taken for granted.

Mrs. Taylor has brought you a few candles because she has heard about the electricity being temporarily shut off. She advises you to store drinking water, and you are filling what empty fruit jars and bottles you can find. As you talk with this good neighbor you are amazed at how strong she is—a little more serious than usual, but energetic and determined. You are very thankful to have her for a neighbor.

But still your mind reverts to Christmas, only weeks away. You stand as if in a trance. How could life change so much from one year to another? Where will you get the courage to be cheerful and make this a happy occasion for your family? You feel as if you are in a deep, black hole with no way out.

While you may not personally have had this nightmare, your experience with dreams helps you to know the sense of relief one would have on waking from it. Fortunately there is food in your cupboard, gas in the car; and your husband and the children are going to work and school as usual.

But don't feel too relieved. The nightmare might still arrive for many of us, and this time in reality.

CHAPTER 2

WHAT IF?

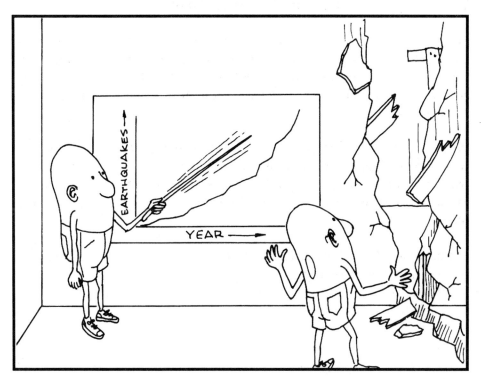

In the 1950's, my family began to heed the counsel to do all we could to learn to become self-sufficient. Over the last 40+ years, none of the predicted major wars, widespread devastating earthquakes, or global financial chaos we prepared for ever materialized. Is there really any reason, then, for me to write this book to encourage you to prepare for possible disasters? Yes, yes, yes and yes!, because disasters of all kinds are on the increase.

Consider the following facts:
According to the U.S. Geological Survey, the number of earthquakes registering 6.0 and higher remained fairly constant up until 1950, averaging 2-4 per decade. The numbers then began increasing significantly (See chart below.) Surprisingly, the increase in volcanic eruptions follows a

very similar pattern. Tornado totals for 1916 through 1998 follow the same pattern, with a dramatic increase during the 1990s.

	Earthquakes	Volcanoes
1920s	3	3
1930s	2	3
1940s	4	2
1950s	9	2
1960s	13	4
1970s	51	6
1980s	86	8
1990s	385	37

We are seeing record-breaking storms, flooding, drought, hot and cold temperatures, as all of our weather becomes more severe. Many times each year, rescue efforts are organized to help in areas of widespread disaster. When will it end? According to Revelation and other books of scripture, as we get closer to the Savior's coming, extreme weather conditions will become the norm, rather than the exception, making the predicted famines inevitable.

Wars and rumors of war have also steadily increased. According to the United Nations reports, violence in 1998 has almost doubled that in 1997.

Disease is increasing, despite modern medical advances. The plague of AIDS has become the leading cause of death for the 25-44 year old male in the U.S. According to Roger K. Young, author of "...And There Shall Be Signs...", "Pfesteria, Hauntavirus, Ebola, Heart Disease, Cancer, Diabetes, Gonorrhea, Syphilis, Super Tuberculosis, Plague, Lyme disease, Gulf War Syndrome....are just a few of the diseases that are running rampant throughout the world. Most have become incurable in that they are, or have become, immune to treatment by antibiotics."

Even though catastrophic events and diseases are increasing, many people live in areas of the country where they are relatively unaffected. Does that mean those people need not prepare for disasters?

A disaster doesn't have to be MAJOR to produce major consequences capable of upsetting normal everyday routines, or even to produce a scene much like the Nightmare Dream mentioned in the previous chapter. There are many disasters that can and do occur in families, neighborhoods, or communities that can be minimized or averted, IF we are prepared.

After all, we've been strongly urged since 1937 (Conference Report, April 1937, p. 26.) to store a year's supply of food and other necessities in our homes, against any one or a combination of the several possible emergencies—unemployment, sickness, strikes, famine, civil disorder, war, and so on. To be unprepared despite the repeated warnings would certainly increase the nightmare quality of the experience.

In the following "What If" scenarios, many of which have actually occurred in my own family or to close friends, try to picture yourself and your family in these same situations. What would you do IF these happened to you?

WHAT IF...you turn the television on to the weather channel and hear that a category 4 hurricane is headed your way. After days of heavy rain, the lake near you is expected to crest within the next several days. What will you do? Consider the following scenarios:

1) It is the end of the month. You are really short of cash. Your 4 credit cards are maxed out and you have only have 1/4 of a tank of gas. To get to safety, you need to travel hundreds of miles to beat the storm and look for a free shelter;

2) You have only one car and your husband needs it to work up to the last possible minute. You need to go to the bank and are not sure how long it will stay open, since the employees also need to get out of town. You decide to take the children and walk to the store to buy food, water and diapers, but as you get close, you see the lines are blocks long. The temperature is in the 90s, and the children are miserable. When you all finally get inside, all the water is gone. The only diapers available are "newborn" size;

3) The roads out of town are backed up for miles and your car's engine is coughing and sputtering. You might be nearly out of gas, but it's more likely that the car really DID need the tune-up you've been putting off for months.

OR...What IF

1) It is the end of the month, but you aren't at all worried, because you have enough cash on hand for emergencies. You always pay off your credit card bills each month, so if you run short, you can always "charge it!" You never let your gas tank get less than half full.

2) You don't need to fight the crowds at the grocery store because you have on hand;

A- A 72-hour kit for each family member, and an emergency kit in each car;

B- A year's supply of the necessary food and personal items your family will need;

C- Because you as a family have a preparedness plan, and a pre-arranged location where you can go to wait out the storm, no one panics;

3) You have your automobile in peak condition, because you faithfully follow your scheduled maintenance program.

WHAT IF...the wind suddenly increases and the balmy summer day turns ugly, as winds uproot power poles and massive 100-year old trees as if they were match sticks. Suddenly, you are without power, even though you are miles away from the worst damage. It is estimated that it will take days for repairs to be made.

WHAT IF...your husband suddenly loses his job? Jobs are scarce, and predictions are that it will take at least 6 months to find something suitable. You could go to work, but your salary wouldn't begin to cover all the bills.

WHAT IF...you are in a drought that has lasted through the 6 hottest months of the year. You have been careful to water only during your few allotted hours each week. Friends in other parts of the state have experienced low water pressure because the drying clay soils have shifted, causing water pipes to burst. Without warning, you find that you have no water at all. When you turn on the television, you find that the town's water main has broken, and that you should expect to be without water for at least 2 days, and that all water will have to be boiled or purified for several days thereafter.

WHAT IF...an ice storm blows through in the night and you wake up to find you are without power. The weather is well below freezing, and the skies are cloudy and threatening. The house is dark and cold, even during the daytime. Ice is so thick that everyone is advised to stay at home for at least 4 days until the weather clears.

WHAT IF...a winter snow storm closes the main roads to your town. Within a few hours, your grocery store tells you it could be as long as a week before they can again get fresh produce and supplies to stock their empty shelves.

WHAT IF...you head to the grocery store for your week's worth of food and other essentials, and then discover you've made a major boo-boo in your checkbook and you are already $500 overdrawn. You have cut up all your credit cards in an effort to get them paid off, so you really have no where to turn.

WHAT IF...you are hurt on the job and won't receive a regular paycheck again for several months?

WHAT IF...you have an accident that totals your car, and even with the insurance money, you must come up with several thousand dollars to find a suitable replacement.

WHAT IF...you work for a company that manufactures winter clothing and camping gear. Because of the unseasonably warm weather this year, sales are at an all-time low. You are advised that in order to survive without layoffs, the company must cut salaries by 10% for all employees, at least until the next season, which is 6 months away.

WHAT IF...a family member dies, and you must take unpaid time off work and buy airline tickets you really can't afford, in order to travel to the funeral...or, what if it's the wage earner in your family who dies? Are you prepared to live without that income? For how long?

I don't know very many people who haven't yet experienced at least some of the above situations. Sadly enough, most of those people were unprepared for the emergencies they faced. Most, however, experienced only a loss of employment. Only those who had been obedient to the counsel to store food were able to survive their time of crisis without fear.

Perhaps for most of us there is still time to prepare, IF we procrastinate no further. Who can say what "emergency" lies just around the next corner???

Why live from day to day...or from paycheck to paycheck? Why not be prepared by getting out of debt, storing a year's supply of basics, buying in bulk and on sale, living from a well-stocked pantry rather than running to the store several times a week? You too can learn to be more self-sufficient, to spend less than you earn, and to choose, store and use the foods necessary for good health.

PEACE—OR PANIC?

It has been my experience that many people will "panic" when starting a program of this type, and assume they need to get prepared all at once. I urge you to be calm. Picture a fire truck pulling up to a fire. Do firemen RACE off the fire truck and frantically run around to get the fire put out? No, they are well-trained to go about in an organized, methodical way to accomplish their assigned tasks. Do WE need to RACE around in preparing for disasters? No, that usually produces an overwhelmed feeling that leads to panic and depression. We need to calmly educate ourselves, come up with a workable plan, and then work that plan. Do firemen work alone? No, they work as a team. Put together your own team so you can share the responsibilities and help each other become as prepared as possible.

HOW WILL *YOU* PREPARE?

There are many ways to prepare for emergencies, some more expensive than others. You can spend many thousands of dollars on prepackaged units of food and other supplies that are designed to be stored away in case of a disaster. Or, you can store the "basics" and learn to use wholesome grains, legumes and seeds on a daily basis. Then, as you save money on the meals you make with your "basics," you can buy the "extras" to round out your storage and provide a wider variety of meals. You can avoid going into debt to get prepared by buying only those things that are essential to keep you alive and in good health, and that will provide a small measure of comfort.

Preparedness is a way of life, not something you do once and forget about it for the next 30 years. A pantry full of nutritious food is better than money in the bank. Exactly what you store and how often you use it is an individual matter, but we each have a responsibility to provide for our families. Stored food "may well be as essential to our temporal salvation today as boarding the ark was to the people in the days of Noah." Ezra Taft Benson

I suggest you begin with the concepts, basic foods and methods outlined in the pages of this book.

WHAT IF?

Gather friends and family together and list here the situations that might occur in your lives and how you can prepare for them.

PART TWO
BUILDING YOUR PREPAREDNESS ARK

Building a "Preparedness Ark" is something everyone can do regardless of circumstances or finances. The amount of preparation will vary, but everyone can do their best with the resources at hand. Everyone **can** do *something* to prepare for the inevitable unexpected events in the future. We can all get out of debt, stock our pantries, learn to live a simpler lifestyle, and be able to produce at least some of the food we eat.

CHAPTER 3

12-STEP ARK-BUILDING PROGRAM

- How to Afford And Maintain A Year's Supply
- Building Your How-To Library
- What, Why, Where, and How to Store
- Water - Storing and Treating
- What To Eat and Why
- Food Preparation Equipment
- The Switch to Stored Foods...
  Recipes To Keep You Healthy
- Keeping Clean - Sanitation
- Energy - Keeping "Comfy"
- Emergency Doctorin'
- Growing, Sprouting,
  and Harvesting
- 72-Hour Kits,
  and Emergency Plans

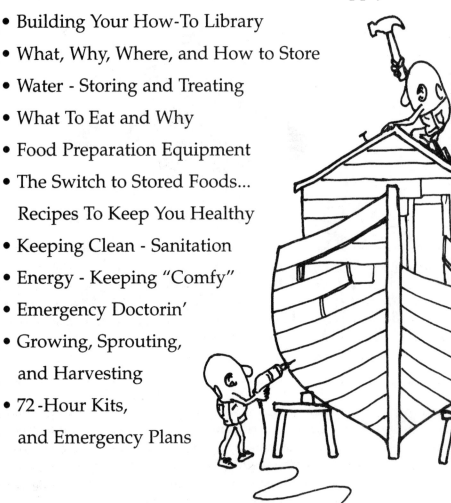

STEP 1

HOW TO AFFORD AND MAINTAIN A YEAR'S SUPPLY

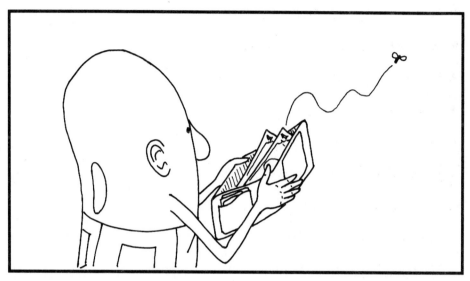

Once you make some basic changes in your spending and saving habits you will find it relatively easy to acquire the basic foods - grains, legumes, and sprouting seeds. When you start incorporating some of these basic foods into your everyday meals, you will save enough money on food to be able to purchase additional food and supplies to help you maintain a well-stocked pantry at all times.

How To Afford Storage

Whether you have a lot of money, or only a little, you CAN be prepared for emergencies. It seems an overwhelming task when one looks at all that needs to be done, but focusing on one or two areas at a time works well for most people. Having less money to spend requires a well-organized plan that usually takes longer to complete, but it IS possible to be well-prepared and self-sufficient on very little money.

Preparedness on a limited budget is best achieved one small step at a time. The 12-step Program outlined in this book will help show you where to begin. Once you decide what to buy and set up your budget, you can watch for sales or bartering opportunities. If having a year's supply of ANYTHING seems like an impossible task, start with the easy things like toothpaste, salt, or cinnamon! It's rewarding to see your level of preparedness increase.

A person with good financial resources has the advantage of being able to buy convenience foods, special clothing, camping and cooking equipment, and supplies that require a minimum of effort to store, set up and use. That person finds it relatively easy to be prepared for any disaster. It has been my experience, however, that the people who DO prepare are most often the ones *without* much extra money. They are the ones who carefully make a plan, set up a budget, and wisely use the money set aside for preparedness to purchase high quality food, basic equipment and supplies. They store inexpensive, wholesome foods — the basics, and use them to create inexpensive meals that supply far better nutrition than the "fast food" meals eaten by the majority of Americans on a daily basis. A year's supply of essential storage foods (365 lb. of grains, legumes, sprouting seeds) costs only about $150 per person!

CHANGE YOUR SPENDING HABITS
1. Decide as a family this year that 25% or 50% of your Christmas will be spent on a year's supply. Many families spend considerable sums of money for Christmas gifts and entertainment. Half of that money would go a long way toward purchasing the basics.

2. Instead of buying new clothing, shop at resale shops or garage sales. Where possible, repair and mend to make your present wardrobe last a few months longer and USE that money saved to buy basic foods. Make all the necessities you can, starting with basic food preparation and moving on to clothing, furniture, etc. (bearing in mind that it often costs more to make clothing and furniture than it does to buy used items).

3. Cut your recreation budget by 50%. Plan activities that do not require money. Play games at home. Get friends together for a potluck dinner

or picnic. Get involved in a service project and give of your time. Serving others as a family gives a more lasting happiness than the "high" of an exciting movie or a day at an amusement park.

4. Decide as a family that there will be no vacation or holiday unless you have your year's supply. Many people could buy a full year's supply of the basics on what they spend on vacation during only one year. Take vacation time and work on a family garden. Learning to work together can be just as much fun, and much more rewarding.

5. If you have boats, snow mobiles, campers, or other luxury possessions and you do NOT have a year's supply, sell or trade one or more and buy essential food and other necessary supplies.

6. Watch for advertised specials in the grocery stores and pick up extra of the items you use that also store well.

7. Change the source of protein in your family's diet. Fiber is sadly lacking in diets high in animal products. Protein from plant sources is less expensive, more nutritious, and easier to digest. Meatless meals, or meals containing only small amounts of meat are easy to prepare from stored beans and grains. Far from being "poor man's food," these basic foods are the best foods on earth.

8. Reduce grocery bills dramatically by buying in bulk. Most food and other items purchased in large quantities will save you from 25% to 50%.

9. Make a commitment to buy only the basics on your trips to the grocery store. Every time you feel tempted by effective advertising to buy cookies, candy, ice cream, magazines, or other non-food items, DON'T! If you really do have the money to spend, buy more of the basics!

10. Change most of your "meat and potatoes" meals to "soup and bread" meals. Creamy bean soups can be made in as little as 3 minutes, hearty soups in only 15. Add whole grain bread and a green salad for a completely nutritious meal. (Contributed in part by Janice Bukey)

"The Lord WILL make it possible, if we make a firm commitment, for every ...family to have a year's supply of food reserves." Bishop Vaughn J. Featherstone

LIVING ON STORED FOODS SAVES MONEY

Let's face it, most monthly expenses are "fixed," meaning that we can't change the amount we spend on them. Others, such as food, clothing, and in some cases, utilities, can be adjusted. Meals made from whole grains, legumes, nuts, and seeds are far less expensive than commercially prepared foods, and are usually a LOT more nutritious.

Start by purchasing 50 lbs. of whole wheat (at a cost of about $17.00, or about 30¢ per pound). Collect recipes using wheat to make breakfast cereals, pancakes, and quick breads. Making a "wheat" breakfast at least twice each week for a month will cost about 35¢ per month for just wheat served as cereal, 50¢ if you add eggs and other ingredients for pancakes, and up to $1.00 for quick breads with added fruit, nuts, etc.

How does that compare to a month's supply of cold cereal at more than $4.00 per box? (One mother told me her family of 4 goes through about 1 box per day, averaging about $20 per month per person, nearly $100 per month for the family!) It will take the same number of pounds of grain to fill you up. With the money you saved on breakfasts alone, you could afford to buy some more breakfast basics, like oats (55¢ per pound), and rice (43¢ per pound). Branch out and buy whole beans (52¢ per pound) to add to your grains.

The money you save in one month will be enough to buy basics to use for the next 2 months. The money you save in two months will be enough to buy basics for 4 months! *Note:* If you're not used to eating whole wheat, the scouring action of *insoluble* fiber, found in most grains, may cause diarrhea. If so, the soothing *soluble* fiber in oats and all beans will help.

Recipes using wholesome, basic foods are essential. Collect enough different recipes and basic ingredients to make a different recipe at every

meal for at least one week. You need only 7 breakfasts, 7 lunches and 7 dinners, for a total of only 21 recipes. You'll find hundreds of my favorites in **Country Beans, Natural Meals In Minutes,** and **1-2-3 Smoothies.**

Once you get your recipes together, you'll find that by just adding a few more basic ingredients to your list, you can vary these recipes to give them a completely different taste. (You can turn cooked rice into rice pudding by adding raisins and vanilla to your storage list, or cracked wheat cereal into a sandwich filling by adding catsup, mayonnaise, dried onions, and dried parsley.)

Choose one storage recipe at a time and purchase all the ingredients needed to make that recipe once each week for a whole year; then start making and serving it. Every week, add another recipe, and in less than 6 months, you can be speeding right along on the preparedness super-highway.

The money saved by buying and using whole beans, grains, nuts and seeds is usually enough to be able to afford to buy all the other necessary supplies and equipment needed.

Start looking for bargains on other products you use regularly. Figure out how much toilet paper you use each week and buy enough for 52 weeks. It's really CHEAP to buy a year's worth of toothbrushes...or dental floss...or toothpaste...or deodorant.

What about candles? They go on sale at up to 90% off after each holiday. If candles were your only source of light, would anyone complain if you burned the wrong scent for the season...or if the candle was decorated for Easter and it happened to be Valentine's Day? I don't think so!

How To Maintain Your Stored Supplies

LAZY INVENTORY PLAN

I'm quite a list-maker, but I don't get a thrill out of knowing exactly how much I have of what item at any given time, so I'll fill you in on my "lazy" inventory plan. Once I figure out approximately how much I need of a particular item, I buy a year's supply (or more) and stack in on a shelf, under a bed, or in a closet. The amount of room it takes is always saved for that item. When I see a hole in that spot, I know it's time to stock up again, so I either go buy it or start looking for sales on it. Be sure to keep soaps, cleaners, fuel and other strong-smelling things away from food.

On my kitchen shelves (and in my refrigerator and freezer), I have all my beans, grains, flours, cereals, nuts, seeds, and dried fruit in clear plastic or glass containers. When a container is empty, I go to my storage shelves for a refill. When I start getting low on an item that I buy more frequently than once a year, I write it on a sticky note and put it in my planner until I get to the store or find a bargain. That's it! It's that easy.

My mother's record-keeping was also very simple. She made a list of the things she used, the amount she stored, when she bought them and how long she thought they would last. This is the form she used:

OUR FAMILY RESERVES

Item Stored	Amount Stored	Date Purchased	Suggested Replacement Date

If you're one who loves to make lists, you can get as detailed as you want. My brother has his huge basement storage room shelves inventoried on a computer spreadsheet. His stored goods are stocked alphabetically, no less! It is great fun to go "shopping" in his basement grocery store! For those of us who live in hot climates and have to store things under beds, in closets, and along walls in air-conditioned bedrooms, that level of organization just isn't practical.

Kristy Carver, a well-organized friend and food storage "nut" like me, does an excellent job of tracking how much of a particular food she uses by writing the date on the lid *when she first opens it*. When that container is empty, she writes down how long it took to use it. She then calculates how many containers her family will consume in a full year.

This method also works well for items like toilet paper, soap, or other personal needs. It takes very little time and effort to get started, and is amazingly easy to maintain. You can choose to restock monthly, quarterly, semi-annually, etc. Kristy uses a spreadsheet to track how much is on hand, container sizes, and how much is needed.

Kristy got cooperation from her family by planning a "food storage" meal once each week. Everyone expected a meal that was slightly different from their usual fare, so the family was prepared to try new things they didn't think they would like...at least two bites! Over the years, tastes have changed, and some of the meals that didn't go over too well are now heartily accepted.

Note: If you haven't yet incorporated basic storage foods into your meals, you won't know how much you would use in a year. I find it easiest to buy enough grains, legumes and sprouting seeds to provide complete nutrition (about 365 lbs. per person per year, or 1 lb. per person per day). (No, these may not be the foods you might *choose* to eat, but they *will* sustain life!) Once you have a supply of those items on hand, you can relax a little. Start collecting recipes (I'm obviously partial to my own!) and deciding how many times each week you will use them. Check out Janice Bukey's method on p. 62 for calculating amounts needed to gather a year's supply of the ingredients in each recipe.

Most people who make the "switch" to using simple, nutritious stored foods, with the addition of fresh fruits and vegetables, *are able to save enough money on grocery bills to buy the "extras"* their recipes call for...like honey, oil, powdered milk, tuna, mayonnaise, olives, soup mixes, peanut butter, canned or dehydrated fruits and vegetables, etc. What a great way to save money and improve your family's health while you gather a year's supply!

There isn't any "right" way to keep track of what you have...just do whatever works for you.

Stock up when you find bargains. I most often do my major "stock up" in the fall. It must be the squirrel in me, but I enjoy doing my "hunting and gathering" when a little of the Oklahoma heat goes south and the weather gets a little cooler. Items stored in my garage have a longer shelf life if I restock AFTER the hot summer is over.

Cooler days are excellent for bottling beans and soups. (On the rare years when I have access to a lot of fruit to make jam, I mash or puree the fruit and freeze it until winter when it's a pleasure to heat up the kitchen.) When turkeys go on sale for Thanksgiving, we buy several, cook them and place the meat in freezer bags to add to our sandwich fillings, taco mix, burritos, and soups.

Form buying clubs and co-ops to purchase large quantities of food and other supplies at a discount. In an organized group, responsibilities for finding the best buys can be shared. One person can find the best prices on beans, another on honey, another on storage containers. Work with other groups to purchase a truckload at a time for best bargains.

Set up a *Bargain Hotline* of those interested in passing on any special bargains they find. If you had 20 people in your group divided into groups of 4 or 5 and you found a great buy on toothpaste at only 47¢ per tube (this actually happened to me recently!!..and it was good toothpaste!), you, as group leader, would call group #1 to pass along the news of your bargain, and assign each of them to call one other group. Each person would only be responsible for calling only 4-5 people. If anyone else found a bargain, they would first call you and you would be responsible for passing it on.

STEP 2

BUILDING YOUR HOW-TO LIBRARY

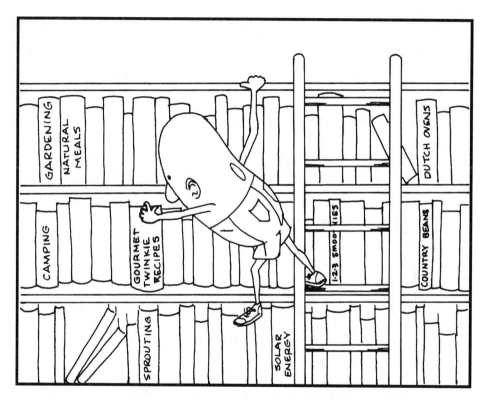

COOKING WITH STORED FOODS

The best recipe books are those that help you learn to use wholesome stored legumes, grains, nuts and seeds on a DAILY basis in recipes requiring very little preparation time. These are the very foods that will provide essential vitamins, minerals and enzymes to build and improve nutrition...for the best health possible. When an emergency arises, you may have to replace fresh fruits and vegetables with dehydrated or canned ones, but your family will transition easily if they're already used to living on the most inexpensive and easy-to-store basic foods — legumes, grains, nuts and seeds.

Country Beans, by Rita Bingham
Soups, Sauces, Dips and Gravies from dry beans in only 3-5 minutes! 400 heart-healthy, cholesterol-free bean and grain recipes using wholesome storage foods. Over 120 recipes using bean flours. Learn how to make "user friendly" beans and low cost meals in 30 minutes or less. Most recipes are gluten-free. $14.95

Natural Meals In Minutes, by Rita Bingham
Learn to cook whole grains in only 15 minutes! Complete storage meals in 30 minutes or less using whole grains and legumes. Includes a variety of sprouting instructions and recipes, and amounts to store. Learn to make Powdered Milk Cheeses in only 3-minutes. Nutritional information provided for each recipe. Nearly 300 low-fat, high-fiber recipes that use stored foods to create delicious, nutritious meals...in only minutes! $14.95

1-2-3 Smoothies, by Rita Bingham
Make your own "milk" from stored grains, nuts and seeds. Delicious, nutritious meal-in-a-glass smoothies made with 100% natural ingredients. Fruit or vegetable smoothies guaranteed to please the whole family. No sugar or preservatives. Recipes are so easy, children can blend their own healthful tasty treats. Excellent for sneaking whole grains into every meal of the day! Includes valuable nutritional information, including a section on Rx Smoothies to help ease or eliminate the symptoms of colds, flu, Candida, sore throats, etc. $14.95

Food Combining, by Rita Bingham
Better Health—The Natural Way. This valuable handbook will help you learn to use and properly combine Fruits, Vegetables, Grains, Legumes, Nuts & Seeds, and fuel your body with the best foods on earth! Complete protein meals—without animal products. Take CHARGE of your health. Enjoy increased energy. Find and maintain your proper weight. Save money on grocery bills. Learn about enzymes, the "spark" of life! Book features a "Natural" Food Pyramid to help you see what foods your body *really* needs, and a Food Combining Chart for best digestion. $7.95

Quick, Wholesome Foods, by Rita Bingham and LeArta Moulton
65-minute video showing step by step, fast, easy techniques to make
food storage into scrumptious meals. This unique training video provides five 15-minute mini-classes on Bread, Gluten, Wheat, Beans and 3-
minute cheeses made from powdered milk (even old milk!). Excellent
for home, church or neighborhood groups. We've made it easy for you
to use basic stored foods. Includes FREE recipe booklet. $29.95

The above books and video are available from Natural Meals Publishing.
To order, call Toll-Free 888-232-6706. In Oklahoma, call (405) 359-1221.

The Amazing Wheat Book, by LeArta Moulton
This book is a MUST for using your stored wheat! Every possible way
to prepare wheat, including gluten (wheat meat) in only minutes, delicious breakfasts, breads, desserts and snacks. Plus how to use herbs and
spices to add a gourmet touch to basic foods and recipes for making your
own seasoning mixes. Includes food substitutions and replacements.
Note: Some recipes contain refined sugar. $15.95. To order, call Toll-Free 1-
800-Herbsetc.

The Food Storage Bible, by Jayne Benkendorf
Shows you how to choose grocery store products to use and store. Quick
and easy reference guide, including products free of harmful preservatives, and how to eliminate the mystery of understanding food labels.
Jayne provides valuable information on diet and health, foods to avoid
and foods to limit. $16.95. To order, call Toll-Free 1-800-580-1414.

15-Minute Lowfat Storage Meals, by Jayne Benkendorf
Learn about the "Fabulous 30" foods. How to store and use them to create meals that are made from healthful, everyday storage foods, low in
fat, high in energy, free of harmful preservatives, and ready in a FLASH!
You'll learn to choose convenient foods. These high-octane whole-food
meals are time-tested. Your family will love them! $14.95. To order, call
Toll-Free 1-800-580-1414.

Cookin' With Home Storage, by Vicki Tate and Peggy Layton
A collection of over 700 food storage recipes. Authentic pioneer recipes for using your most basic storage items. Many recipes to help in using dehydrated foods. Home Remedies like Grandma used. Natural Beauty and Personal Care section. Emergency Baby Care section. Preparedness section, including where to go for preparedness products. *Note: Some recipes contain refined sugar and refined flours.* To order, call (435) 835-8284, or (435) 835-0311.

GENERAL PREPAREDNESS
Making The Best of Basics
Family Preparedness Handbook by James Stevens
This #1 best-seller is full of BASIC how-to information. If you want to learn how to prepare for survival living, this book will help you with charts, lists, resources and down-to-earth "basic" recipes. James' motto is "Store What You Eat, Eat What You Store, Use It Or Lose It!" $21.95. To order, call (210) 695-4200.

Don't Get Caught with <u>Your</u> Pantry Down! by James Stevens
How to find preparedness resources for the unexpected AND expected! A comprehensive reference guide to the preparedness industry. Includes profiles of over 5000 businesses providing in-home food storage and emergency preparedness products for prudent, practical people in uncertain times. $29.95. To order, call (210) 695-4200.

The Sense of Survival, by J. Allan South
This handbook is one of the most comprehensive guides on the market for emergency preparedness! The first of three sections is about the likely possibilities, such as what to do before, during and after natural disasters, a nuclear incident, or a biological or chemical attack. The second section describes how and where to acquire the necessities of life: emergency kits, food storage and nutrition; equipment, water; sanitation; care of infants; gardening, and much more. The last section includes a first aid manual and primer on growing and using herbs. $15.95. To order, call Toll-Free 877-767-4381.

Skills For Survival, by Esther Dickey

This book teaches skills that would be essential in emergencies and in learning to be self-sufficient, whether you live in the city or on an acreage in the country. Esther's motto "Use it up, Wear it out, Make it do, OR DO WITHOUT, is well illustrated in this comprehensive book. Full of information like beekeeping to better health, gardening to grinding grain, storage techniques to seed selection.

At 83 years old, Esther is a true pioneer in every sense of the word. She still gathers most of her food from her yard and garden and prepares all her own nutritious meals. Her lifelong interest in good health and proper diet has encouraged hundreds of thousands of people to store and use only the best quality foods and to be prepared with the basics so they can "Be Prepared...and Fear Not." $16.95 ISBN 0-88290-093-5. Horizon Publishers.

GERM AND INFECTION CONTROL AND TREATMENT
The Authoritative Guide To Grapefruit Seed Extract, by Allan Sachs, D.C., C.C.N.

Researchers are discovering the power of grapefruit seeds, which provide safe and inexpensive raw materials to support a quiet revolution in the control of problematic germs. From Candida, to traveler's illness, sore throat, gum disease, flu, colds and beyond, this product is earning a reputation as the most versatile mainstay of herbalists around the world — a breakthrough in alternative treatment and in water purification. Dr. Sachs is a pioneer in the field of clinical ecology and the creator of many herbal formulas used by holistic practitioners throughout the world.

HOMEOPATHY
As overwhelming numbers of Americans lose faith in modern medicine, this is the right era for us to learn about this time-honored method of healing, whose preparations are obtained from animal, vegetable and mineral sources. Why not try a homeopathic, safe remedy as an appropriate treatment for strep throat, colic, morning sickness, tension headaches and avoid the need for habit-forming laxatives? The following list includes my favorite books:

Homeopathic Medicine At Home, by Maesimund B. Panos, M.D. and Jane Heimlich

Homeopathy For Children, by Henrietta Wells, MCH.RSHom

The Complete Guide to Homeopathy, by Dr. Andrew Lockie and Dr. Nicola Geddes

Let Like Cure Like, by Vinton McCabe

An excellent website for valuable information on health, as well as homeopathic books and supplies and a free newsletter is: health@elixirs.com, or http://elixirs.com. Or, call Kathryn Jones, Health Counselor, at 1-800-390-9970. Her consultation fees are very reasonable. She can get you started on how to be your own doctor, whether you want to doctor only cuts, bumps and bruises, or to move on to allergies, toothaches and broken bones.

HOME REPAIRS
Thousands of dollars are spent each year on home repairs that could be turned into less-expensive do-it-yourself projects. All that is needed is a selection of good books, some essential tools, and a little practice to boost confidence.

It might help you to make a checklist of repairs that should or most likely **will** need to be made within the next year. Then visit your local library and check out How-To books and videos. When you find one you like, purchase it. If you know someone who has the knowledge, ask for help or volunteer as an apprentice.

I believe we can figure out how to do almost anything if we just set our minds to it and give ourselves time to think through the problem.

GARDENING
Chemical fertilizers and pesticides are like antibiotics - they kill EVERYthing. It is the earthworms and tiny "critters" that replenish the nutrients in the soil and keep it "loose" so roots can travel freely. If your soil is compacted, it needs organic fertilizers, lots of "mulch" and a fresh

supply of earthworms and composted kitchen food scraps. Again, a trip to the library is in order. In only one year, you will see a major improvement in how much better your garden plants look and taste.

We added one bucket of earthworms to a "wormless" garden that would hardly grow weeds and ended up with lush plants and worms in every shovel full of dirt. It usually takes about 3 years to create a good organic garden with healthy plants that are virtually bug-free and very disease-resistant.

It is important to collect seeds that can be used year after year. Most seeds are hybrids, and the seeds from what you harvest cannot be replanted to obtain the same plant. Heirloom or Heritage seeds can be ordered from the following internet sources:

> www.seedsblum.com/
> www.heritage.com.au/
> www.heirloomseeds.com/
> www.simpsonsherbfarm.com/index.html
> www.richters.com/faqs/faqs63.html
> www.verrillfarm.com/saveseed.html
> www.brandywinefarms.com

Check with your county extension service for varieties that grow best in your area.

Learn to grow "up!" The vines of tomatoes, melons, and all legumes will cling to strings or poles or stakes, leaving the ground free for other crops.

FOOD PRESERVATION

Learn to preserve excess food. Often there is "free food" (or nearly free) available at the end of a growing season, or on rare occasions at grocery stores, such as berries, apples, pears, melons, and bananas. Learning to take care of what you grow or gather can save you money and will certainly increase your level of self-sufficiency. Bottled beans and vegetable soups are very inexpensive and easy to prepare. They make almost "instant" meals, even without heating.

See Country Beans, p. 157 for instructions on how to use a pressure canner to preserve a wide variety of bottled beans and soups. You'll love the results! Beans and bean soups are easy to prepare and far better tasting than any commercial product.

If you live in an area of the country with abundant fruit, you'll need to get information on dehydrating and freezing. Home dehydrators are fairly inexpensive and provide an excellent method for preserving food in a small space.

WATER STORAGE AND PRESERVATION

You won't need a book on how to store and purify water, but you will need to make an educated decision when choosing where to store water and in what containers. Whether you choose 2-3 litre pop bottles or plastic containers from one to 55 gallons, be careful to specify only "food grade" plastic.

Best Prices Storable Foods (972-288-0262 or http://web2.airmail.net/foodstr2) carries Softank™ Storage Systems in 30 gallon or larger. As the name implies, it's a soft plastic tank that sits flat on the floor. Excellent for under beds, in attics, or outdoors. Very durable, even in direct sunlight.

For information on how to purify water for storage, or for drinking, call toll-free 1-888-232-6706 for the free brochure "GSE—The all natural treatment for drinking water."

Check out internet sites for dealers who supply water purifiers. I like the Safari Outback (about $30), from Cotton's World of Water (http://welcome.to/watersavers, or 1-888-865-8916). Mention Natural Meals Publishing and receive a 5% discount.. The Sweetwater Guardian (about $50) and the Katadyn pocket filter (about $250) are also excellent water purifiers.

STEP 3

WHAT, WHY, WHERE, AND HOW TO STORE

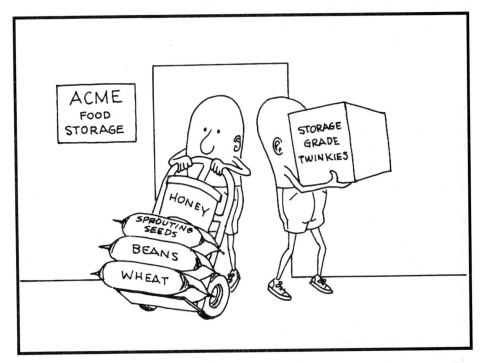

The Seven Survival Foods
Grains, Legumes, Sprouting Seeds, Honey, Salt, Oil,
and Powdered Milk (opt.)

These seven versatile foods can be combined, flavored, seasoned, modified and disguised to create amazingly delicious meals with an almost never-ending variety of tastes and textures. I find it simply astounding that a believable meat substitute can be made from wheat...or milk...or soybeans!

Doesn't everyone love Campbell's cream soups? For only pennies, you can make a delicious substitute...without milk, wheat flour, or fat...in only 3 minutes...from **BEANS!**

Did you know that milk doesn't *only* come from cows? A tasty, nutritious milk substitute can be made from grains, seeds, or beans...and again, it takes only minutes!

"Veggieburgers" and other meatless patties really *don't* taste like meat, but I prefer them to meat because I know how much better than meat they are for me. The whole grains, legumes and seeds I use to create great-tasting "burgers" are free of the harmful growth hormones, antibiotics, and other chemicals fed to most animals. Besides, there isn't ANY fiber in meat, no matter how much chewing it takes to be able to swallow it!

What about FRESH food storage? Unless you can grow your own garden year-round, you WILL need to find a way to get the essential enzymes, antioxidants and phytochemicals found in fresh, raw fruits and vegetables. The process of sprouting changes dry grains, legumes, and other seeds into a "live" state, activating dormant enzymes and making available thousands of micronutrients to heal and nourish the body. It also moves them into the vegetable category on the food pyramid, thereby fulfilling the body's need for "fresh" food.

When enough "live" foods are eaten, the body's immune system is brought into balance, and DNA is repaired. That's all the body needs to be able to heal itself of minor OR major illnesses. Our magnificent bodies were designed to heal themselves, but the typical American diet of meat, refined sugars, refined grains, and chemical-laden "fast food" doesn't supply any of the "raw materials" necessary for healing. The overuse of antibiotics further weakens the immune system, forcing the body into a state of disease. Eating wholesome foods (that just happen to store well!), and learning to pay attention to the body's distress signals, will help you fight off illness before it gets to a critical state that requires medical attention and antibiotics.

Learning to be creative with whole foods can save you money, improve your health, and quite possibly totally eliminate the need for doctors, except for emergencies like broken bones and the need for stitches. For more information, see **Food Combining,** *Better Health—The Natural Way.* This book is a mini-nutrition manual to help you find out what it takes to heal the body, stabilize hormones, regulate metabolism to achieve proper weight, teach you how to prevent and even reverse illnesses such as heart disease, cancer, arthritis, and more! Order information is in the back of this book. For more information on nutrition, enzymes and fiber, see Step 5.

STORAGE FOODS TARGET

To get the best possible nutrition, start with the basics. The 3 most beneficial categories are placed in the bullseye—the center of the target. Start with these and add the others if and when you can afford them.

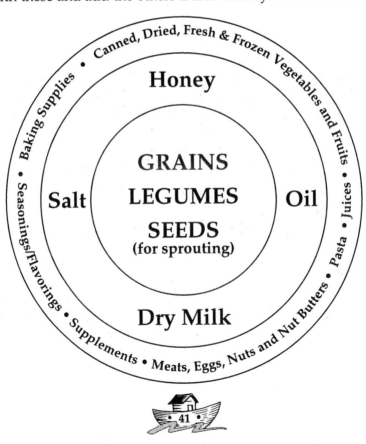

1. GRAINS

WHEAT, the staff of life, is indeed a versatile grain. Used in appetizers, main dishes, salads, snacks and desserts, wheat adds flavor, texture, and protein as well as many important vitamins and minerals. Fiber in the American diet is a popular subject these days, and whole wheat is one of the best tasting and easiest to use sources of fiber available. Cracked wheat cooks in only 15 minutes and can be added to almost any recipe.

If you are just beginning to use high-fiber whole grains, start by including small quantities of cracked wheat or whole wheat flour each day in your diet. Consuming grains in large quantities can cause diarrhea because of the insoluble fiber they contain. (Note: adding soluble-fiber beans slows down the transit time and stops the problem in its tracks!)

Wheat Allergies
Many people are becoming allergic to wheat. Whether this is because of the frequency of use, the many chemicals used in crop production, or because of some other undiscovered cause is not clear. Many people who have experienced strong reactions to wheat have found that they can tolerate sprouted wheat. Sprouting increases the enzymes necessary for digestion, so it is a possibility that some food allergies are related to an insufficient quantity of digestive enzymes.

The best way to avoid food allergies of all types is to use a wider variety of foods and to practice a 4-day rotation plan. Use the foods most likely to cause an allergic reaction only every 4th day and only in small quantities. (These foods are: milk, eggs, wheat, soy and corn.) It also makes good sense to use sprouts, unprocessed whole grains, and organically grown foods whenever possible. Most people, after following this type of diet for a few weeks, find they can better tolerate the offending foods when eating out, or with friends, or when they just can't stand being so regimented for even one more MINUTE!

Many who are allergic to wheat can easily tolerate rice. While it is always best to use whole grains (as in brown rice), those unused to whole grain fiber may need to start by using white rice, then mixing in quantities of brown rice, gradually eliminating white rice. Brown Basmati rice is our family favorite, even for those who used to like only white rice. Like cracked wheat, cracked rice takes only 15 minutes to cook, as compared to long grain rice that traditionally takes 45 minutes to cook. Rice can be used in any recipe calling for whole or cracked wheat.

Triticale, spelt and kamut are all members of the wheat family, but are often tolerated by those allergic to wheat. They can be used in place of wheat in any recipe. Rye adds a tasty flavor to any bread recipe. Whole oats and barley, also excellent sources of nutrition and fiber, can be substituted in some recipes. These are a great addition to any soup. Millet makes an excellent breakfast cereal or pilaf.

When a recipe calls for wheat flour, a Gluten-Free (GF) flour mixture may be substituted. (Usually, extra leavening in the form of eggs or egg substitutes are added to replace the gluten found in wheat.) I find the commercial varieties very white, processed-tasting and pasty, so I have developed my own "healthy" mix using brown rice flour, whole bean flour and other ingredients. See index for the GF Flour Mix recipe, or purchase GF Flour at your favorite health food store.

2. DRY BEANS (LEGUMES)

Beans, peas and lentils are one of the best food bargains on the grocery shelves. They are important staple foods for well over half the world's population. Many of us in the United States are just now learning to appreciate their hearty goodness. Most of us are familiar with pinto and kidney beans and homemade split pea soup, but there are many other, almost limitless ways to use legumes.

With advance preparation, beans can be added to many last-minute meals. Beans can be cooked, sprouted, cracked or even ground to a fine flour; then frozen until ready for use to preserve the nutrients.

Legumes are born mixers as well as meat extenders. They can be mixed with other vegetables, used to "beef" up a salad, or served as dips and sandwich spreads. Legumes are a rich source of protein, iron, calcium, phosphorus, thiamine and potassium. When combined with grains, they supply all the amino acids necessary to form a complete protein.

BEANS IN HISTORY

Simple Foods and Better Health
Throughout history, many people have experienced improved health when they were forced to live on more simple, basic foods; their health improved and they were even able to feel better while eating smaller quantities of food. One reason for their improved health is that commercially prepared foods are almost always filled with chemical additives, colorings, flavorings, and depleted of the unstable part of the food that allows it to spoil. Whole foods should always be our *first* choice, since foods in their more natural state are more easily utilized by our bodies.

Poor Man's Meat
Dry beans are among the oldest of important staple foods and have long been known for their low cost and high nutritional value. Often called "poor man's meat," a pound of beans, when cooked, will make about 9 servings, compared to 5 servings per pound of cheese and up to 4 servings per pound of meat, poultry or fish.

24 Carat Meals
Beans were once considered to be worth their weight in gold — the jeweler's "carat" owes its origin to a pea-like bean on the east coast of Africa. They also once figured very prominently in politics. During the age of the Romans, balloting was done with beans. White beans represented a vote of approval and the dark beans meant a negative vote. "How to Buy DRY BEANS, PEAS, and LENTILS," U. S. Department of Agriculture.

The use of beans dates back to as long ago as 7000 B.C., with the remains of lentils being found in the Egyptian tombs dating back more than four thousand years. Soybeans and mung beans have always been highly regarded by the people of China and India.

In Cuba, the black bean is a favorite. Mexico favors all sizes of kidney beans. Navy beans, cranberry beans and white beans are most popular in the New England states. The South and Southwest prefer red beans, pinto beans and black-eyed peas. With this rich heritage of ideas and the availability of such a wide variety of beans, we can enjoy beans of a variety of flavors, colors and a multitude of ethnic seasonings.

BEANS IN THE KITCHENS OF TODAY

Cooked Beans
Cooked, mashed beans can be added to soups, sauces, patties, loaves, casseroles, "meat" pies, sandwich fillings, dips, etc. Dry beans can be soaked, cooked and frozen, or soaked and pressure bottled. I use both methods, but prefer bottled beans as they are the fastest to prepare and the easiest to use. Also, they taste most like the canned beans available at the grocery store.

Cream Soups and Sauces
ALL cooked beans can be puréed to make "almost instant" cream soups or soup base, and can be served as a "cup-a-soup" for a quick, high protein meal in minutes. They need no added fats to make them creamy, rich and thick.

3. SPROUTS

Because of our need for fresh "live" food and the enzymes and healing properties these foods contain, it is essential that a variety of sprouting seeds be an absolute essential part of every home storage program.

SPROUTS ARE VALUABLE SOURCES
OF VITAMINS, MINERALS, AND PROTEINS
Sprouted grains and beans increase in vitamins A, B and C, E, and K. Riboflavin and folic acid increase up to 13 times the original amount present in dry seeds. Two of the most important amino acids necessary for the body to manufacture proteins are lysine and tryptophan, which are increased significantly during sprouting. Vitamin C increases up to 600% in some cases. (**Great Tasting Health Foods,** by Robert Rodale.)

England, which is dependent on outside sources for fresh fruit to supply vitaminC has made special studies that indicate that about 1/4 c. of peas sprouted for 48 hours supply the daily vitamin C requirement. Research conducted at the University of Minnesota reports large increases in the B vitamins in sprouted wheat.

Leafy, green sprouts such as alfalfa, radish, clover, sunflower and buckwheat lettuce and wheat grass, contain a rich supply of chlorophyll, a valuable source of vitamin A and protein. Research conducted by Dr. Charles R. Shaw, M.D., Professor of Biology at the University of Texas System Cancer Center in Houston, indicates the possibility that chlorophyll prevents formation of carcinoma (cancer) in mice. "The chlorophyll appears to exert its inhibitory effect (up to 99 percent effective) by interfering with enzymes which activate the carcinogens." This information applies to uncooked sprouts.

Nutrients and volume increase during sprouting, but calories do not, making sprouts a good low-calorie addition to any meal, or even as a meal by themselves. Many people use a variety of sauces and dressings added to a generous serving of various sprouts for a super delicious, nutritious, sprout meal or snack. Many children love to eat cool, crisp, clover and alfalfa sprouts by the handful.

It is best to serve a wide variety of sprouts to ensure a balanced diet since no one type of sprout contains all the essential nutrients to maintain good health. My favorites are adzuki, alfalfa, hulless barley, buckwheat, clover, garbanzo, soy and mung beans, lentils, hulless oats, peas, quinoa, and wheat.

4. NON-FAT DRY MILK

To some, the mere mention of this "powdered milk" evokes disapproval. Let's be objective about this. If the milk is properly prepared and served iced, good quality powdered milk is acceptable by itself, but virtually undetectable when used in cooking and baking. It is high in protein and low in calories. Besides, if you were in a situation where you couldn't buy fresh cheese, sour cream, cream cheese, cottage cheese, or yogurt, what would you do? Using easy-to-store dry milk powder, you can make your own dairy products. See **Natural Meals In Minutes**, page 115 for recipes.

Milk is included in many recipes for those who choose to include milk in their diet. Non-instant milk tastes better and is usually cheaper than the grocery store variety of instant milk crystals. Powdered instant milk is a good choice, but is usually more expensive. In my recipes, I always use non-instant. If you use instant powdered milk crystals, amounts used in these recipes will need to be changed. For the brand I normally use, three cups of non-instant milk powder + almost 4 quarts of water = 1 gallon of liquid milk. Adjust recipes to your particular brand of milk powder.

If you're allergic to milk, or have other reasons for not drinking it, try one of the many alternative milks. Our family health is improved when we eliminate milk (and all dairy products), so I sometimes buy milk made from soy, rice, oats, or almonds. I usually make my own milks from all of these, plus other versatile grains, nuts and seeds like barley, sunflower, or sesame—and in only 3 minutes! (I'm a big fan of 3-minute recipes and 15 minute projects!! and explanation marks!!!)

5. HONEY

Honey is not just another high-sugar content food. It is the most natural sweetener, and it stores forever. It is usually the only sweetener I use, because sugar supresses the immune system. I don't know anyone who can afford to be unprotected from the constant daily barrage of viruses and bacteria. Before you bite into a candy bar or a gooey brownie, or guzzle a "Big Gulp," ask yourself if your health is good enough to open yourself up to whatever invaders you'll encounter within the next few hours...or whatever may already be lurking inside you, waiting for a chance to get the upper hand!

If you choose to use sugar, it can be substituted in most recipes using the following conversion: 1 c. honey = 1 1/4 c. sugar and 1/4 c. water. These recipes have been specially developed to use honey, and a number of changes have to be made. Maple syrup can be used in place of honey using equal proportions.

Note: Raw, unfiltered honey has been determined unsafe for babies less than 1 year old.

6. SALT

While not actually a food, this combination of sodium and chlorine is one we have come to depend on to enhance the flavor of our foods. It is not essential to the body, as there is enough naturally-occurring salt in foods from the plant kingdom to adequately meet dietary needs. Many people learn to live without it and quickly learn to enjoy the real taste of the food.

Salt is an excellent preservative and most of what I store is for use in making sauerkraut and other preserved vegetables, and for preserving fish from my freezer if the electricity should be off for an extended length of time.

7. OIL

We need fats—the ones occurring naturally in whole foods. Fats are made up of fatty acids—saturated, polyunsaturated, and monounsaturated. The liver uses saturated fats (found in animal products, vegetable shortenings, and some foods from the plant kingdom like coconut and palm) to manufacture cholesterol. Polyunsaturated fatty acids are found in corn, soybean, safflower and sunflower oils. Monounsaturated fatty acids are found mostly in olive, peanut and canola oils. Most foods, however, contain a combination of all of the above.

Good Fats—Bad Fats
The changes that occur when polyunsaturated oils are hydrogenated (hardened into a solid like margarine and shortening) cause increased cholesterol. It won't do much good to cut meat or egg consumption to lower cholesterol if you're still using margarine or shortening. I'm often appalled when a recipe that serves only 6 people calls for 1-2 sticks of margarine. Whether it's a casserole, bread, or dessert, you can either eliminate the fat all together or substitute a healthful oil instead.

All oils are 100% fat, and full of calories. Most oils are very highly processed. The only oils we really NEED are those that occur naturally in small amounts in all foods, such as fish, whole grains and legumes, and in higher amounts in avocados, olives, nuts and seeds.

Since most of us choose to use oil anyway, choosing the best oils will have the best effect on our health. Look for cold-pressed oils, meaning the seed, grain, or fruit containing the oil is pressed at room temperature to extract the oil, rather than using heat and chemicals to separate the oil from the food. These are usually found at health food stores. At the top of the list is flaxseed oil, but it has a very short shelf life and must be kept refrigerated or frozen. Once opened, all cold-pressed oils (except olive oil) should be refrigerated because they quickly go rancid at room temperature.

The flaxseed is rich in omega-3 essential fatty acids, magnesium, potassium and fiber and is agood source of zinc, B vitamins and protein. It has a pleasant, nutty taste that makes the whole or ground seeds an excellent addition to cooked or cold cereals, pancakes, muffins, salads, etc. The oil, when cold-pressed, is rich in fatty acids that are known to lower cholesterol and triglyceride levels. Purchase the oil from a health food store and keep frozen or refrigerated. Barlean's is my favorite brand. A surprising amount can be added to most drinks without any off-flavor. **Note:** While on vacation recently, I bought Barlean's flaxseed oil . It tasted like cod liver oil! If it doesn't smell *pleasant*, it isn't fresh.

Olive oil is next on the list, and an excellent choice, because even cold-pressed olive oils have a long shelf life. Again, less refining means a more nutritious product, but even olive oils that don't say "cold-pressed" are still healthier for you than any of the others. Heading on down the list, my next choices are safflower, sunflower, corn and soybean. I used to use mostly canola oil, made from the rapeseed, but recent research indicates it may be cancer-causing (most likely due to the way in which it is usually processed). The key is to look for oils that are monounsaturated.

I do not use any oil in my bread, because the bread is moist without it. I prefer to spread real butter on an occasional slice of bread and thoroughly enjoy it. I NEVER use margarine because it is loaded with cholesterol-producing trans-fatty acids. Because of the extra processing involved, I do not store butter or margarine powders. Learning to omit or limit the fats and oils you use will be better for your budget, your health *and* your waistline.

FLAVORINGS are an important storage extra. I most often use vegetable or meat based bouillon or soup bases, and other ordinary cooking spices and seasonings. Liquid extracts or oils like vanilla, almond, coconut, cherry, mint, strawberry, etc., are compact and very helpful in making drinks, baked goods, etc., when fresh fruits are not available. Dry seasoning mixes such as Italian, taco, barbecue and enchilada are helpful, but not essential. All of these seasoning mixes can be made at home without preservatives and little or no salt.

Other foods that are nice to have on hand:
Dry Yeast, Baking Powder, Baking Soda
Tomato Juice
Pineapple Juice
Fruit Juice Concentrates (frozen or shelf-stable)
Blackstrap Molasses
Nuts and Nut Butters
Sesame Seeds
Sunflower Seeds
Dry Parmesan Cheese
Dried Fruits - Dates, Raisins, Prunes, Figs
Herbs and Spices
Nutritional Supplements (I recommend Juice Plus+)
Canned or bottled fruits and vegetables
Canned or bottled beans
Flavorings
Seasonings

What About Baby?

Babies need to eat, too! How could a baby or a small child survive the switch from commercially-prepared baby food to stored whole grains?

Refined cereals and overprocessed fruits and vegetables are often the *cause* of constipation in infants. To remedy this, bean flour can be cooked in a dry saucepan, microwave or oven until slightly browned. These flours will then cook in only 1 minute, when added to water. By adding reconstituted, cooked bean flours (seasoned to taste) to cereals, vegetables and even fruits, infants and children can be fed meals which are more nutritious and unlikely to cause constipation. Brown rice flour is also excellent to add to foods for children.

Our children were all raised on "real" food—rich in fiber and nutrients—and much of it raw. Actually, children *thrive* on high-fiber foods if they are started on small quantities and their tolerance is not exceeded. It is a huge mistake to feed children only "pre-chewed" baby foods that have been peeled and cooked and processed beyond recognition. When available, use soft raw fruits such as bananas, pears, peaches, plums and apricots, and avocados. Lightly steamed carrots, potatoes, sweet potatoes, and all green veggies are excellent. Make sure to serve dark-colored foods, as they most often contain the highest amounts of nutrients. Our daughter Kimm teethed on "green trees" (broccoli tops). The stem made a great handle, and she munched her way through many treetops. At 15, she still loves broccoli.

Soy milk, used in many formulas, can be made at home and added to many foods for children, especially cereals. Other excellent milks can be made from raw sunflower or whole brown sesame seeds, almonds, brown rice, barley, or oats. These milks (except soy milk) are low in protein, but mother's milk is only 1 1/2% protein. Carrot and other vegetable juices are also excellent milk substitutes.

Wheat grass and wheat sprouts can be added to infant formula to increase the intake of vitamins C, A and E. Any type of sprouts could be liquified and fed to a baby until he is old enough to chew food well.

Nutritious broths that add minerals, vitamins and proteins can be made by pouring warm water over whole grains and allowed to stand overnight, then poured off and placed in a bottle or cup.

Wheat pudding can be made from steamed cooked wheat, mixed in the blender with milk (or alternative milks) and honey. Millet, oats, barley, and brown rice also make an excellent pudding.

Dr. Lendon Smith, "The Children's Doctor," recommends Sesame Milk as a replacement for those with milk allergies or to use when milk is not available. According to Dr. Smith, unhulled "sesame seeds contain ten times per weight the amount of calcium in milk." One cup of sesame seeds makes a nutritious milk substitute, high in protein, calcium and magnesium.

To make *Sesame Milk*, toast 1/2 c. unhulled sesame seeds in 300°F oven for 20 minutes. Combine seeds with 2 c. water and 1 T. honey in a blender and process for 2 minutes, or until seeds are liquified. Repeat with an additional 1/2 c. raw seeds seeds and 2 c. water. Strain through a large strainer, using the back of a large spoon to press as much liquid as possible from the mush. Refrigerate milk and use within 3 days.

Designing A "USER-FRIENDLY" Storage Program

Other things besides food and drink may be needed in an emergency situation. To be independent and self-sustaining we should store items for comfort, health, cleanliness, and well-being. Even if we ourselves should not find the need for some of these stored items, it would be a satisfying experience to be able to respond to a call from others for help. In fact, helping others always imparts a satisfaction—even a zest for living. This would probably be even more noticeable in a time of emergency, when we would all need to remain positive and be productive.

Rather than store what someone else stores, why not take a notebook and walk through each room, making a list of supplies used in that room. Calculate what you would need to function in that room with and without electricity. So you don't get overwhelmed in a hurry with the kitchen, start with a bedroom. You would need extra flashlights, batteries, candles, a battery-operated or wind-up clock. Whoever lives in that room will need sturdy clothing and shoes. In baby's room, you will need warm sleeping wear, extra diapers (preferably cloth), etc. When you get to the bathroom, think *survival*, not what you normally keep on hand. Make sure you have a good first aid kit. What will you do about sanitation? (See Step 8.)

When it comes to medicines, first make an effort to get healthy. Good food, exercise, and preventive measures will eliminate the need for most medicines and start you on the road to completely eliminating minor illnesses. If you have a health condition that can't be corrected quickly, make plans to have the medicines you need on hand. Most insurance companies won't cover "a year's supply" of medicines for storage purposes, so be prepared to pay full price.

Even the kitchen that seems so overwhelming isn't all that bad if you adopt a plan like mine to live on soups, sprouts and quick breads if I can't buy or grow fresh fruits and vegetables. How much fuel does it take to cook a quick bean soup? Not much! Check out Step 6 for information on alternative cooking equipment.

ARK-STOCKING CHART

Stocking your "ark" with the basics doesn't take much money compared to what we normally spend in a year's time. It does require careful planning though, to buy, store and use power-packed, nutritious whole foods if you're not used to them. Plan now to get "back to basics" and learn to use these items year-round, supplementing with fresh foods as available.

Item	Adult (Male or Female)	Child (to age 6)
Wheat	165 lbs.	75 lbs.
Other Grains (oats, barley, corn, rice, rye)	80 lbs.	35 lbs.
Powdered Milk (or alternative)[1]	16-60 lbs.	24-60 lbs.
Legumes (beans, peas, lentils)	60 lbs.	25 lbs.
Honey (or substitute)	60 lbs.	30 lbs.
Salt	5 lbs.	2 lbs.
Fats (olive oil preferred)	2 gal.	1 gal.
Seasoning herbs, spices, mixes	**	**
Bouillon (or miso, etc.) to flavor soups & sauces	enough to flavor 22-35 gal. water	enough to flavor 10-15 gal. water

Item	60 lbs.	30 lbs.
Sprouting Seeds (to eat and plant)	*equivalent to 5 servings per day	*equivalent to 5 servings per day
OR Vegetables and Fruits (dehydrated/bottled/canned) (if you don't plan to sprout)		
Water	14 gal.	10 gal.
Water purification - NutriBiotic GSE	4-8 oz.	2 oz.
Yeast (also starters to ferment soy, sourdough, etc.)	4 lbs.	1 lb.
Baking Supplies (leavening agents, carob chips, etc.)	*	*
Medical (first aid, and medications)	*	*
Fuel (for cooking, lanterns, etc.)	2 wk. supply	2 wk. supply
Cooking equipment (stoves, pans, grinders, etc.)	*	*
Sanitary Supplies (toilet paper, and personals)	*	*
Personal Care (toothpaste, toothbrushes, dental floss, shampoo, hair spray, and deodorant)	*	*
Laundry soap, Clorox bleach, household cleaners	*	*
Nutritional Supplements (I recommend Juice Plus+)	*	*
Camping Gear (tents, tarps, backpacks, coats)	*	*
Bedding (sleeping bags, blankets, pillows)	*	*
Scriptures and Legal Documents (waterproofed)	*	*
Individual and family birth certificates, shot records	*	*

* The starred items should be stored on an as-needed basis. Certain areas of the country require preparations for winter, others for hot weather. Some people can grow gardens year-round, so would not require nutritional supplements or as many sprouting seeds. Store the types of vegetables and fruits you use in preparing basic preparedness recipes. The space available for storage will determine the types of foods you can store. Most people are limited on space, so only the most basic essentials can be stored.

**Experiment with recipes to find out what kinds of seasonings you like, then store a year's supply of them. For instance, if it takes 6 bouillon cubes (2 T.) to season a soup or a casserole for your family, assume that you will use some type of bouillon at least 4 days a week, throughout the year. You would need to store about 21 cups of powdered bouillon. Choose recipes wisely so you can vary the recipe to use either vegetable, chicken and beef bouillon. If you use taco or other seasoning mixes and you use them once a week, buy 52 packets of your favorite brand. OR, purchase seasonings to make your own (and be sure to include the recipe!).

[1]A U.S. government study on maintaining nutritional adequacy during periods of food shortage suggests that 64 quarts, or 16 pounds, of dry milk powder per family member per year, will maintain minimum health standards. (Ensign, March, 1997, p. 71.)   What are the alternatives? The reason for storing milk is to provide a source of calcium. All beans (especially soy), dark green, leafy vegetables, and sprouts are good sources of calcium. Powdered soy milk is a good replacement.

Choose wisely when purchasing storage foods, paying special attention to nutritional needs for your individual family members. Store foods that are free of harmful preservatives and chemical additives. Give your body the best chance possible to be healthy. (Check out **The Food Storage Bible** by Jayne Benkendorf, listing about 5,000 safe foods from the grocery store.

Prioritize your storage. What would you absolutely NOT want to live without? Next to my food, I'd rather have toilet paper, tampons, sanitary napkins, etc. I'd even eat all my food raw (sprouted) if it came down to a choice between cooking fuel and sanitary supplies!

WHAT ELSE SHOULD BE STORED?

Where possible, store a year's supply of fuel for heating, such as wood, coal, etc.

I have crocks, and extra salt to make sauerkraut and to salt and brine meats and vegetables.

Money is exceptionally nice to have on hand!! Plan to have at least $20 for each person's 72-hour kit in small denomination bills and coins. Save at least a month's salary in the bank or another safe place.

A battery-operated radio (and spare batteries) is essential for times when the power is out, especially during a time when you need to hear a message on an emergency broadcast station. Change batteries when daylight savings time changes each year. (This is a good time to change the batteries in your home smoke detectors too!)

Plan to spend several days throughout the year on "dry runs" so you will know where your supplies are stored, and how to use them.

WHAT ABOUT FRUITS AND VEGETABLES?

The Benson Institute suggests that 370 quarts of pickled, canned, or bottled fruits and vegetables should be stored for one person for one year to supply essential vitamins and minerals. This is roughly 1 pound per day per person. (Having Your Food Storage and Eating It, Too, BYU Press, Provo, Utah, 84602.) Sound like a lot? For a family of 5, this would amount to 1,850 quart jars of produce each year! Few people have access to that much produce, let alone that much storage space.

If no canned, bottled, or dehydrated fruits and vegetables are stored, then each person should store at least 60 pounds of a variety of seeds that can be *sprouted and eaten raw*, for fresh salads and greens. For cooking, store at least 60 pounds of legumes (beans, peas and lentils). Why only 120 pounds, if each person needs 1 *pound of vegetables* each day? The volume of dry beans, peas, lentils and other seeds increases at least three to four times during the sprouting process.

If you're one of the lucky few who has a fairly good supply of bottled or dehydrated fruits and vegetables stored, then consider storing the following amounts for variety and better nutrition:

30 pounds per person of seeds to be used in salads or as salad greens (sunflower, pumpkin, peas, red, black and green lentils, alfalfa, clover, buckwheat, radish, adzuki, garbanzo, quinoa, wheat, oats, and mung bean).

It is important to try different varieties of sprouts and the different methods of preparing them; you will then know what types your family enjoys and which ones to store.

WHAT SEEDS DO THE BINGHAMS STORE?

Most storage plans, if they recommend sprouting seeds at all, suggest storing about 10 lbs. per person. I know how important "fresh" foods are, so I store far more than most people for the three of us still at home. Since we have wheat allergies, I store and use less wheat and more other grains and legumes.

In addition to bottled and dehydrated fruits and vegetables, I store the following quantities of seeds (in pounds) for sprouts to be **eaten raw** (in addition to wheat): Sprouting Barley-25, Rye-5, Mung Beans-30, Alfalfa-20, Adzuki-20, Peas-10, Lentils-30, Quinoa-10, Clover-5, Sunflower-50, Buckwheat-25, Garbanzo-10.   For sprouts to be **cooked,** I store: Lentils-30, Garbanzo-50, Pinto Beans-50, Navy or Small White Beans-60, Soy Beans-25, Mung Beans-40, Kidney Beans-20.

Because sprouts are such a good source of nutrition, I use them to supply necessary nutrients and consider most of the rest of our foods merely enjoyable "bulk."

For delicious recipes using sprouts at every meal of the day, see **Natural Meals In Minutes.**

HOW LONG TO STORE

Sprouting seeds need to "breathe." If they are stored too long in an oxygen-free environment they smother in their own carbon dioxide. We can't breathe this byproduct and live; neither can seeds. How long is too long? Sprouting experts say 2 years is too long. I successfully sprouted some wheat that had been nitrogen-packed for 9 years, but was unsuccessful in sprouting seeds stored in a gallon jar for only 3 years. There have been success and failure stories on all kinds of seeds and storage methods. The key seems to be to buy a small amount and test the seed before purchasing and storing large quantities. If it doesn't sprout, don't store it.

I baked with some wheat that wouldn't sprout and ended up with "brick muffins." Using the same kind of wheat that DID sprout, I made light, fluffy 100% whole wheat muffins. The moral is - living seeds perform better than dead ones!

Sprouting seeds need to be "aerated" every year. That doesn't mean opening the lid and stirring the seeds; the seeds needs to be dumped out of their container, then poured back in. Since carbon dioxide is heavier than oxygen, it stays at the bottom, so stirring doesn't get rid of it, nor does it add fresh air for oxygen.

HOW TO PROTECT AGAINST BUGS

The purpose of taking OUT the air in stored foods is to prevent weevil and other crawley things from eating more than their share, so you end up with hulls and carcasses. The safest, most effective pest control for grains and small seeds that will be used for sprouting is to add food-grade diatomaceous earth while filling containers. Distribute evenly and coat ALL the seeds. Merely pouring the powder on top does not work.

According to J. Allan South, in **The Sense of Survival,** diatomaceous earth is a white, powdery substance made up of the interior spiny skeleton of small marine creatures whose soft body parts have decomposed, leaving the remaining skeletons that accumulate on the ocean floor over thousands of years. Geological processes bring these layers to the surface where they can be mined and used for filtering systems and pest control. It does not produce a change in taste and it is not nutritionally harmful. Besides, all traces of this fine powder are eliminated in the soaking and rinsing process of sprouting. (In fact, it is an ingredient in many toothpastes.)

Many gardeners sprinkle this powder on their plants. When a bug comes along and ingests this skeleton, the spiny parts in the diatomaceous earth tear up its intestinal tract, and it DIES.

Add the following quantities to all seeds that will be used for sprouting:
>9 cups per 55 gallon drum
>1 cup per 6 gallon bucket
>2 1/2 T. per gallon
>1/2 tsp. (rounded) per quart

A 5 lb. bag containing about 40 cups of diatomaceous earth costs only about $10. The cost of this valuable protection is only about 12 1/2¢ per 6-gallon bucket and about 2¢ per gallon!

COCKROACHES
Boric acid kills cockroaches. It is the principle ingredient used in nearly all commercial roach traps, powders and liquid solutions. Put no more than 1/2 tsp. in one place. Deposit in dark, narrow inaccessible areas where roaches usually hide.

Most beans can be stored without any special treatment. Unlike grains with vulnerable crevices or soft nuts and seeds, beans carry a hard, protective outer shell. I have never had bugs in whole beans. Lentils and peas, however, are not so well protected and DO need special treatment.

OXYGEN-ABSORPTION PACKETS
Small packets filled with natural materials that absorb oxygen are being used to remove the air from stored foods. The packets come in a sealed bag and must be kept air-tight to prevent them from absorbing oxygen in the room. Once the sealed bag is opened, enough packets are

removed to process about 12 cans. If the package is not resealed, with all air forced out, the remaining packets will absorb oxygen from the room, and will not be effective in removing oxygen from your sealed foods.

One small packet (D-300) per gallon can or jar (or quart jar), and one to two large packets (D-750) per 5- to 6-gallon bucket creates an oxygen-free environment so that bugs and/or their eggs cannot live to reproduce. It is very discouraging to open a 5-gallon bucket of improperly-stored grain to find each kernel riddled with holes where weevil have eaten away the germ and left a nasty residue.

Oxygen-absorption packets are best to use when storing foods such as dehydrated fruits and vegetables, and nuts, seeds and legumes that will not be used for sprouting.

One preparedness store uses oxygen-absorption packets to remove air AND adds diatomaceous earth on the sprouting seeds they sell in sealed gallon cans. This is an extra measure of protection and is a good idea, as long as you remember to date the containers and open them after one year to aerate. Covering the can with a plastic lid will provide enough protection after opening seeds stored in this way, even over a period of several years.

DRY ICE
Dry ice kills most adult insects and larvae, but merely treating a container of food with dry ice will probably not destroy the eggs or pupae unless the container in which you place your food has a tight-fitting lid with a gasket designed to be air-tight. (This is the method we successfully used for over 20 years, before we started using gallon metal cans.)

"Pour 2" of wheat into the bottom of the container. Add slightly crushed dry ice; then fill with wheat." Three ounces of dry ice is recommended for 36 pounds (or one 5 gallon bucket), "eight ounces for 100 pounds, or one pound for each 30 gallons of stored grain. Seal the containers loosely for 5 to 6 hours (to allow air to be driven out); then seal them tightly." (*Essentials of Home Production & Storage*, published by The Church of Jesus Christ of Latter-day Saints, Salt Lake City, Utah.)

HOW TO KEEP TRACK OF WHAT YOU STORE

A friend of mine, Janice Bukey, still has her 6 children at home, and is much more organized than I ever was about keeping track of her food storage. This is her inventory list of stored items for 1 year (for a family of 8).

Janice came up with this inventory record by listing all the ingredients used in each of her storage recipes, then multiplying those ingredients by the number of times she wanted to serve that particular recipe throughout the year. Items are marked with the date purchased as they are put onto the shelves.

GRAINS
Cornmeal-60 lb.
Rice-200 lb (40 cans)
Oats-75 lb (30 cans)
Flour (White)-100 lb.
Wheat-1,500 lb. (300 cans)
Cream of Wheat - 6 boxes
BAKING
White Sugar-50 lb.
Brown Sugar-25 lb.
Honey-40 lb.
Molasses-3 bottles
Oil-15 gallons
Cornstarch-2 boxes
Baking Powder-3 lb.
Baking Soda-5 lb.
Yeast-12 pkg.-6 lb.
Salt-24 boxes
Shortening-12 cans
SOUPS
Onion-20 boxes
Cr. Celery-25 cans
Tomato-25 cans
Cr. Mushroom-50 cans
Cr. Chicken-25 cans
BEANS
Lentils- 15 lb.
Pinto-80 lb. (3 cases)
Red-80 lb. (3 cases)
Split Pea-5 lb.
White-25 lb. (1 extra case)

Pink-20 lb (1 extra case)
Instant Soup-6 cans
VEGETABLES
Green Beans-100 cans
Peas-25 cans
Corn-25 cans
Potato buds-8 cans
Dried onions-2 cans
Dried carrots-2 cans
Dried peppers-2 lb.
Alfalfa seeds-5 pkg.
Tomatoes-350 cans
Tomato sauce-100 cans
Tomato paste-25 cans
FRUIT
Applesauce-25 jars
Peaches-75 cans
Fruit Cocktail-25 cans
Pineapple-15 cans
Mandarin Oranges-10 cans
Raisins-10 lbs.
PASTA
Spaghetti-50 lb.
Macaroni-50 lb.
Egg Noodles-20 lb.
Lasagna-5 pkg.
CANNED MEATS
Tuna-35 cans
Chicken-35 cans
SPICES
Cinnamon-2 lg.

Oregano-3
Pepper-4 lg.
Onion Salt-2
Dry Mustard-2
Italian Seasoning-2 lg.
Chili Powder-2 lg.
Garlic Salt-1 lg
Tabasco-1 bottle
Basil-2
Paprika-1
Garlic Powder-2
Worchestershire-2 bottles
Vinegar-2 gallons
Bouillon, beef-4 jars
Bouillon, chicken-5 jars
Bouillon, vegetable-2 jars
OTHER
Dried Milk-3 cases
Orange Drink-3 cases
Peanut Butter-12
Green Chiles-25
Syrup-12
Parmesan Cheese-6
Jello-50
Dressing-25
Ketchup-6
Pickles-5

BONUS ITEMS
Mixes, Baking Items
Juices, etc.

WHERE TO STORE

We store most of our food in gallon containers that we've processed at the Family Canneries belonging to the Church of Jesus Christ of Latter-day Saints. These canneries are found across the United States. However, these facilities are no longer capable of supplying food to groups outside of their own membership, due to the increased need to help members in other countries devastated by severe weather and other disasters, and the increased use by members working to get their own year's supply. The canneries are, however, acting as resources to help others find products and supplies to form their own canning groups.

Metal cans are no longer being used. Instead, easy to store and reusable mylar bags are used, holding about 20% more than the gallon cans used previously. Bags are filled and an oxygen-absorbing packet inserted, then they are sealed and placed in cardboard boxes (5-6 to a box). These boxes stack very well, up to 10 high. We place them under beds (most often stacking them 2-deep and discarding the bed frames), in closets, and from floor to ceiling along the wall in larger bedrooms. Storing food in a garage is acceptable only if temperatures rarely get above 80°F in the summer. Foods stored at high temperatures lose most of their nutrients and enzymes in a very short time. Fiber and protein are about the only important things which remain in improperly stored foods.

YOU WANT ME TO PUT IT WHERE???

There are those who insist they would NEVER use their stored foods as end tables, or put a curtain over a wall lined with food storage. I'd rather not have bags and boxes in my living room, but if it comes to having no other place to store food, I would find a way to make it look functional, even attractive!

Weeding out the "extras" in your homes or apartments can free up lots of space. My Mother's old motto applies here... "store the best, and leave the rest." Decide what your priorities are and then look at what you're willing to sacrifice to have peace of mind and the security of knowing you're well prepared.

• Store in durable containers that are best for your area. In dry climates, metal cans work well. In humid areas, cans will rust quickly. Use only containers that will keep out air, moisture, and pests.
• Storage area should be clean, cool, dark, dry, well-ventilated, with low humidity for longest shelf life.
• Store foods away from cleaners and other products that may affect the flavor and taste of food.
• Do not place metal, glass or plastic on or against cement or dirt floors or walls because they will absorb moisture and odors. Place a piece of wood on the floor or against walls. Metal or wooden shelves are best.

Stored foods last longest at cool temperatures, up to 70°F. In areas of the country where the outside temperature stays relatively cool in the summer, food can be stored in a garage. In Oklahoma, where I live, I store food outside during the winter and use it up before summer, replenishing my supply again in the fall when the temperature drops. Those lucky enough to have basements usually have no problem finding room for stored foods.

If you're not one of the lucky few, and need to store your food inside, here are a few other options:

UNDER BEDS...
• Boxes holding 6 gallon cans or 5 mylar bags fit easily under most beds. 10 boxes (60 cans, or 50 bags) will usually fit under a twin bed. We have often stacked the boxes two high, covered them with a dust ruffle, and placed the mattress right on the boxes, neatly hiding 20 boxes (120 cans). I always have more than a year's supply of stored grains and beans, so I most often use those items to hold the beds.
• Boxes holding 12 quart jars of canned beans, fruit, vegetables, soups, or even dry beans and grains, nuts and seeds, will also easily fit under beds. Cases of canned vegetables from the grocery store also fit well under beds.

IN CLOSETS...
• Boxes of gallon cans, jars, canned goods, etc. can be stored on the floor of any closet. If the children in your house are like mine, storing boxes

on the floor of their closets and under their beds cuts down dramatically on the number of things they can "stuff" there.
• Many houses have deep closets that will accommodate a row of gallon cans in the back. Now that our children are mostly gone, we have an extra closet that is filled from floor to ceiling with labeled boxes. This involves a "storage shuffle" now and then, but within just a few minutes, I have the item I need.
• Storing seasonal clothing and extra bedding in the attic or garage or storage shed makes room for another row or stack of food in every closet, including the linen closet.

AS FUNCTIONAL FURNITURE...
• Wood veneer boxes over five gallon cans or buckets of wheat could be used as end tables.
• Put a skirt around a card table with storage underneath.
• Uniform containers against a wall could be covered and padded and used for seating. If you've always wanted a window seat, give this one a try!

IN THE REST OF THE HOUSE...
• In bathrooms, there is usually lots of room for items like toothpaste and deodorant, with room to spare for a few more cans or bottles of food!
• Under desks. Only so much space is needed for knees and feet. One or more boxes usually fits nicely in the remaining space.
• Kitchen. Nearly all of my cupboards are filled with clear plastic containers (one quart or one gallon size). I like to see what I have to use, so I empty my stored beans, wheat, etc. into the see-through containers. In my kitchen I have shelves set aside for whole grains; another for beans; flours, cracked or ground cereal grains; pasta; dried fruits, seeds and nuts; smoothie add-ins like protein powders and grain milks. At least a 3-month supply of food will fit comfortably in most kitchens if you plan carefully and get rid of non-essential items. (Needless to say, there's no space inside for extra gadgets or fancy dishes. Those get moved to the outside shelves in the garage!)
• Laundry room. My handy husband built a shelf above the cupboards, next to the ceiling, for single gallon cans of things I use most often.

• Attics. Things not affected by extreme temperatures are clothing, bedding, paper goods, and objects of metal, wood, glass, plastic and leather.
• Under stairways. Odd-sized or oversized equipment can be conveniently stored in the unused space under the stairs.

Like a squirrel storing nuts, I look for spaces all through the house to hide food. When I find a particularly good bargain or have a little extra money to stock up, we give up one wall in our bedroom and stack food from floor to ceiling. It's amazing what will fit on only one wall.

WHERE TO STORE HIGH-FAT NUTS AND SEEDS
Shelled nuts and seeds, such as almonds, walnuts, filberts, sunflower and pumpkin seeds should be stored in a refrigerator or freezer in glass or plastic containers, or double zip-loc freezer bags. Their fat quickly goes rancid, even though you may not notice a flavor change, and rancid fats are carcinogenic.

FLOURS , CRACKED GRAINS and LEGUMES
Any grain or legume or seed that is cracked or ground to a flour immediately starts to lose nutrients and will become rancid after only a few months. I don't have refrigerator space to store everything I crack or grind, nor do I have the time to grind everything just before I want to use it. Therefore, I compromise and store my commonly-used flours and cracked legumes and grains in quart or gallon containers on my kitchen shelves, using them up within 2-3 months.

STEP 4

WATER

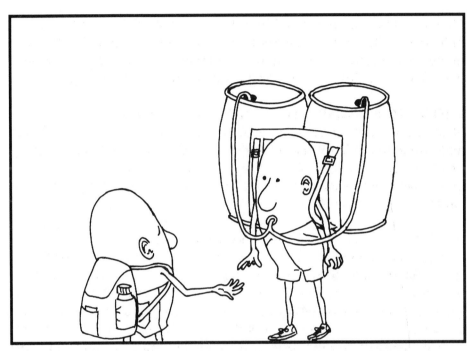

If we have not stored water, how will we rehydrate dried fruits, vegetables, grains and legumes? What will we drink? Water makes up over half the volume of our blood, which carries food elements to every living cell. In an emergency our need for water will be greater than our need for food.

Water is essential to life. The radiator in your car won't run on coke, tea or coffee; neither will your body. Water isn't just something you should drink to quench thirst. Water is *vital* to the proper functioning of your body. People who have been deprived of water have died within a few days, while others with an adequate supply of water have survived for weeks and sometimes months without food.

Water brings valuable oxygen and nutrients into our cells. It carries away carbon dioxide and other waste products, and cushions and protects important body organs such as the brain, spinal cord, and lungs. Water helps to keep the body temperature normal.

Nearly three-fourths of the body is made up of water. Some of that water is used up or eliminated (in urine, sweat, etc.) and should be replaced regularly. You lose 8 to 12 cups of water each day. Drinking less than that amount can damage the body and cause constipation.

NO FOOD, NO PANIC

People who have never gone without food, except perhaps for short periods during mild illnesses, frequently view the possibility of doing so with horror, almost with panic. But there is no justification for this reaction, for it is possible to go without food for many days without any ill effects as long as one has water. For example, many people can go without food for 2 to 3 days and feel fine, as long as they have adequate water.

A friend of mine was happy and energetic after not eating for six days. I have read of people who claim to have been without food for periods ranging from 23 to 102 days and are still healthy.

If we have sufficient food stored, we may not need to go without food, but it is reassuring to know that a person in normal health could still go about his work if only water was available.

Far from dreading abstinence from food, some seek it. Some claim physical benefits from going without food; others abstain for spiritual reasons.

Whatever the reason for going without food, as long as we have water we can relax and know that we will survive for a considerable length of time. Hence if we have stored the minimum amount of water needed for our family, if we know of other local sources, and if we are aware of small ways to conserve water, we can feel relatively easy about this area of survival.

NORMAL WATER CONSUMPTION

The amount of water we use in our homes has increased tremendously over the years. When my mother was a child, they didn't waste water. It had to be carried up in buckets from the ditch in front of the house. Sudsy wash water (using lye soap) was saved to scrub the porches and floors or to douse over cabbage plants to rid them of bugs. Greasy dishwater went to the hogs. Saturday-night bath water from the tin tub (in which more than one person had bathed) was carried out and dumped on the lawn or trees.

Water which had been used to rinse out the milk buckets was poured on the geraniums in the window, and mineral-rich whey from cottage cheese provided fertilizer for plants in the yard. A measured amount of water went into the dish pan or washbasin. There was no waste of running water to get the desired temperature, hot or cold.

Meanwhile, the demand of plant life for water was minimized by frequent cultivation of garden rows to bring up the water, while a mulch of grass clippings and leaves around trees reduced evaporation of water.

POSSIBLE WATER SHORTAGE

What could cause a water shortage? It could be a drought, as prophesied in the scriptures. Earthquakes or bombings could break water lines and disrupt service. Nuclear fallout or contamination from bacteria could render normal supplies unusable.

Temporary extreme water shortages in parts of the United States have silenced our automatic washers, dishwashers, garbage disposers, toilets, showers, and sprinkling systems. But those who stored drinking water and a minimum amount for household use had no need to fear.

When we lived where we relied on a well for our water, we were without water for days at a time when tornadoes or windstorms cut off the electricity needed to pump the well water to the surface. During periods of drought, like the one we experienced in Oklahoma during the summer of 1998, some towns were without water for days. After several summer months without rain, the clay soil dried and shifted, causing pipes and water mains to burst. People who refused to heed the warnings suffered greatly without water, especially on days when the temperature was over 100°F.

Many who have been through severe water shortages have been concerned enough about this natural resource to conserve water even when it was plentiful. During our recent 3-month period of water rationing this summer, a friend encouraged us to put a 5-gallon bucket in each tub and to put it under the faucet while we waited for warm water. I was amazed to find that we wasted about 2 to 4 gallons, not counting the amount we used to get clean! This amount was more than enough to water the garden, flowers and shrubs in between our twice weekly watering turn.

I was so shocked at the amount of water wasted every day that we plan to continue using this method to help do our small part to conserve this precious resource.

News reports indicate that many water treatment plants are already at peak capacity, with the need for even more water growing rapidly. More and more chemicals must be used in order to purify the water more quickly. How long can we continue to have a "land of plenty" if we don't do our part to conserve water?

WATER STORAGE

At a normal rate of consumption it would be difficult to store sufficient water to last for, say, a year. In the expectation and hope that normal supplies would not be cut off for more than about a two-week period at a time, we should store as an absolute minimum, one quart a day for drinking for each adult to cover such a period.

Twenty gallons for each family member would be a safer figure, on the basis that, while this would not last very long, should the emergency be prolonged one would hope to obtain water from other sources before the storage supply was exhausted.

CONTAINERS FOR WATER STORAGE

Bottles of heavy odorless plastic with tight-fitting caps are preferred for storing water. Use only containers that are used or made to hold food or water.

Do not use plastic milk bottles, as they deteriorate and begin to leak within just a few months. Plastic soda bottles are excellent and are easy to carry in a 72-hour kit. Glass jugs or bottles with screw tops can also be used.

Metal containers tend to give water an unpleasant taste. Preparedness stores carry collapsible plastic 1-5-gallon water containers. Where space permits, fill 55-gallon drums with water and equip them with an inexpensive hand pump.

EMERGENCY SOURCES OF WATER SUPPLY

Bottled water, stored canned fruit juices, water in home hot-water tanks and toilet tanks, would help meet the need for liquids. For those on wells, generators, hand pumps, and cisterns would be useful.

ACTIVITIES WHEN WATER IS SCARCE

You can help to reduce the need for water as well as seek to increase the supply. When water is scarce, keep quiet to reduce perspiration. Note that anything that acts as a laxative may deplete the system of moisture. Smoking heightens the need for fluid. Carry a clean button or pebble in your mouth to decrease the sensation of thirst.

If you are outdoors, unprotected from the sun, dig a trench two or three feet deep running east and west (preferably when it is cool), and lie down in the shade during the heat of the day. After being thirsty for a long time, when you find water avoid nausea by drinking only small amounts at a time. Since the skin will absorb water, clothes can be wrung out in undrinkable water and placed on the skin.

U.S. Department of Agriculture Bulletin No. 77 (Home and Garden), p. 315.

COLLECTING RAIN WATER

In an emergency you may need to know how to collect rain water. Scout troops have used the following method: Spread out clothing over sticks or limbs about 6" above ground; shape a sag in the middle of the cloth and put any kind of clean container under the lowest part of the sag.

Most of the water will funnel to this sag and collect in the container. Palm leaves or similar large leaves added along the edges of the clothing will increase the area of the collecting surface.

FINDING WATER

Even more "know-how" is required to find water in the ground. One way is to use a solar still.

In the desert you can get up to three pints of water a day from a bowl-shaped hole in the ground and a piece of clear plastic over the top with a weight in the center and a container underneath. (See diagram on page 73.)

Heat from the sun will cause moisture to condense on the bottom of the plastic and this will drip into the container. Moisture condenses even faster if you drop water-holding desert plants under the plastic. Even impure water, or salty water in the bottom of a boat, can be made pure by this method of vaporizing and condensing."

SOLAR STILL

Dig a pit 1' wide by 3' deep; put a shallow container in the center. If possible, rig a tube from container up to the edge of the pit and stretch clear plastic over pit, with a rock in the center to form a cone directly over container. (Split cactus stems laid around inside will improve yield.)

Any kind of water poured around pit will help. Solar heat evaporates water that will condense on plastic and drip into pan. Draw water through tube to avoid disturbing still. Make several stills, if these are your sole source of water.

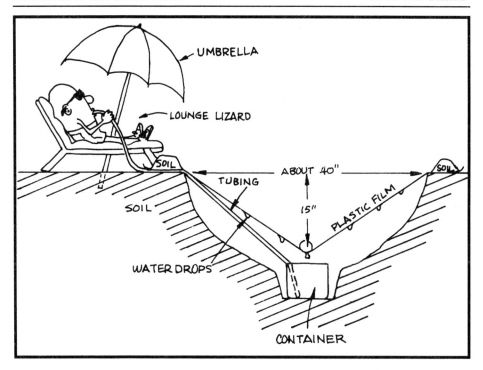

CLARIFYING MUDDY WATER

When water lines are cracked or broken, water is often dirty. If you have to use this water, or if you are collecting muddy water from streams or rivers, it must be clarified to remove physical pollutants using one of the following methods:

- Let stand for 12-24 hours, allowing sediment to sink to the bottom of the container, then dip or carefully pour water into another container, being careful not to stir up the sludge at the bottom.
- Strain through a fine cloth such as a cloth diaper, linen dish cloth, tight-weave tablecloth.

Boil clarified water for at least 10 minutes.

PURE WATER

Regular tap water is usually loaded with chlorine and other harmful inorganics, often making its taste too nasty to drink! Purchase bottled water (tastes good but is not always pure), or a system designed to filter *and* purify. I prefer a system that uses reverse osmosis along with a carbon filter designed to eliminate impurities larger than .2 to .5 microns.

To purify water that has been stored for a while, or that may be contaminated (from rivers and streams, or unsafe water supplies in foreign countries), I add 3-5 drops of Nutribiotic® GSE (grapefruit seed extract) to each glass of water, 20-30 drops to each gallon. This all-in-one antibacterial product is also an excellent household cleaner for toothbrushes, vegetable/fruit or meat/poultry wash, good for sterilizing dishes and utensils, cutting boards and any other "germy" surface.

Healthcare professionals worldwide use this liquid concentrate as nutritional support for individuals with certain health concerns, such as sore throats, colds, and flu. It is excellent as a dental rinse, throat gargle, ear rinse, nasal spray, facial cleanser and scalp treatment. This product is a MUST for every home to help eliminate bacteria the *natural* way. GSE is 100% effective on Strep, Staph, Salmonella, E. Coli, Candida, Herpes, Influenza, parasites, fungi and travelers' diarrhea.

Every 72-hour kit should contain a small bottle of NutriBiotic GSE, or "Traveler's Friend," for water treatment or to counteract the effects of drinking impure water or eating contaminated foods. Every food storage program should have at least a 2 oz. bottle of GSE. No kitchen or medicine chest is complete without the 4 or 16 oz. bottle.

This is truly a miraculous product! It is completely *natural* and without any side effects. A 2 oz. bottle costs only $10.95, contains 1260 drops and safely purifies up to 126 gallons of water. For information on this versatile product, call 1-888-232-6706.

FILTERING WATER

I use a household filter to remove the chlorine and other yukkies from our city water. If you're likely to go camping or don't want to use the grapefruit seed extract, check out internet sites for dealers who supply water filters.

My favorites are the Safari Outback (about $30) from Cotton's World of Water (http://welcome.to/watersavers, or 1-888-865-8916. Mention my name and receive a 5% discount.), the Sweetwater Guardian (about $50) and the Katadyn Pocket Filter (about $250).

HOW MUCH WATER TO STORE

Water is heavy and takes up a lot of valuable storage space. It is recommended that each person store a 2-week supply of water, about 20 gallons - two quarts per day for drinking, one for cooking, and one quart for cleaning and bathing. If you live where water can be collected (near a river, lake or stream), you may be able to simply store containers to collect water, and keep on hand the equipment and/or supplies for purifying it.

STORAGE CONTAINERS

Make sure the containers you use are safe. Large drums that used to contain chemicals or petroleum products would not be safe for storing drinking water. Plastic containers containing carbonated drinks are safe. Bleach bottles are not. Milk or water bottles purchased from the grocery store are safe, but are not heavy-duty enough for long-term storage.

When purchasing plastic containers, buckets or barrels (up to 55 gallons), be sure to ask for "food grade" plastic. Make sure you store a hand pump or siphon to be able to access large containers of water.

Best Prices Storable Foods (972-288-0262 or http://web2.airmail.net/foodstr2) carries Softank™ Storage Systems in 30 gallons or larger. As the name implies, it's a soft plastic container that lays flat on the floor. Excellent for under beds, in attics, or outdoors. Very durable, even in direct sunlight.

HOW LONG TO STORE

Storage time is not important, as long as you have some way to purify the water that will be used for drinking. Again, grapefruit seed extract is the most reliable, most compact product to have on hand.

WHERE TO STORE

Two- to three-litre bottles filled with water fit nicely under beds. They can be placed on the floor of closets and in crawl spaces. They can be stored in attics or garages. Larger containers can be stored outside, in garages or attics (be careful not to overload your ceiling joists).

We keep some small water containers near our 72-hour kits and store the rest in 55-gallon drums. Since we live where the summers are HOT, we store all our water outside and reserve our inside storage space for perishables.

STEP 5

FOOD

What Does YOUR Body Really Need?

Every body needs REAL food, RAW food, WHOLE food. Why?

In 1997, the United States spent $1 TRILLION on health care—just in hospitals and doctors' offices. That's $3,000 for every man, woman and child. We also spent staggering amounts on nutritional supplements in health food stores. So, are Americans the healthiest people on earth?

In comparing the United States to 227 other countries, it ranked 29th in infant mortality and 46th in life expectancy!! That means that people in 28-45 countries spend far less on health care, have far better health and live longer lives than Americans, according to Dr. Ted Morter, author of Dynamic Health.

The USDA food pyramid recommends 6-11 servings of grain per day, and most of those servings are eaten in the form of processed grains (pasta, pizza and breads). Yet, the majority of nutrients necessary for good health and prevention of cancer, and virtually all other diseases, come from fresh fruits and vegetables, NOT from processed grains.

Do you feel healthy, or do you have chronic aches and pains and frequent illnesses that require prescription or other drugs? Would you like to feel better? Could you use more energy without relying on caffeine or other stimulants? Do you worry about getting cancer, diabetes, arthritis, or other degenerative diseases? Is your health good enough to handle whatever stress or disaster might cause you to have to live exclusively on stored foods?

Switching to REAL foods is the first step on the road to better health. What are REAL foods? Foods from the plant kingdom, as close to fresh-picked as possible. Raw foods are the best of all foods, because they contain the ingredients necessary to nourish AND heal the body.

RAW FOODS
Enzymes are the "spark of life" present in all UNCOOKED (raw) fruits, vegetables, grains, legumes, nuts, seeds and even meats! Every chemical action and reaction in the body requires an enzyme. The nutrients in foods are "locked" and cannot be broken down into small enough particles to be utilized by the body unless a special "key" is provided—enzymes!

Besides aiding in the digestion of food, enzymes repair cells within the body. The body makes a specific enzyme to repair the heart, one to repair the kidneys, and so on.

Only a small amount of each enzyme molecule is required to break down these foods. The remaining portion is then sent to the "enzyme bank" until it is called upon to break down foods that don't have their own active enzymes, such as cooked foods.

ENZYMES ARE DESTROYED AT 130 DEGREES F.

Americans eat MOST of their food cooked. Some don't eat ANY raw fruits, vegetables, or sprouts on a daily basis. Enzymes begin to die at 118°F and are completely destroyed at 130°F. Cooked foods lack these absolutely essential molecules. When a body isn't FED enzymes, it cannot do a good job of MAKING enzymes or of breaking down foods into usable molecules.

This may sound like a simple problem, but what happens when the body can no longer make sufficient enzymes? Indigestion is first on the list. We are a nation plagued with indigestion, but that is only a minor part of our ailments. Cooking foods (except lightly steaming or stir-frying) kills the very enzymes all foods NEED in order to be broken down small enough to pass through the minute pores of the intestines into the blood stream.

When we eat fresh foods that are past their prime, or are overcooked, cell REPAIR cannot take place. Imbalances are created and the body begins to weaken. The immune system doesn't have what it needs to fight illness. We set ourselves up for all degenerative diseases, including cancer and arthritis. In a talk by Dr. Joel Robbins, noted biochemist, the U.S. Surgeon General is quoted as saying that "70% of all deaths related to stroke, heart disease and cancer are preventable through diet." The body IS capable of making repairs to damaged cells to lessen or eliminate disease. Recent research shows that whole, raw foods, complete with enzymes, are the key.

What's the best way to start getting a good supply of enzymes when storing dry beans, seeds, grains, and canned fruits and vegetables? When available, make sure to eat "live" fresh fruits or vegetables at every meal and for snacks. At other times, substitute lots of fresh, leafy or crunchy sprouts. They're cheap, easy to grow and require no special preparation.

STORING WHOLE FOODS

WHOLE foods are just that - whole! If wheat has had the outer hull taken off, the wheat germ and the wheat bran removed, and bleached to produce white flour to make the melt-in-your mouth cakes, cookies, pastries, fluffy white pancakes, or boxed instant breakfast cereals, it's not WHOLE! If brown rice has been stripped of its fiber to produce white rice that is easy to store, it's not WHOLE.

WHY ARE WHOLE FOODS IMPORTANT?
Americans have the most abundant food supply in the world, but we are far from being the healthiest people in the world. Why? It's what we DO to our foods that makes the difference. We eat the highest percentage of cooked, processed, refined foods of all "civilized" countries.

These processed foods are in every grocery store and nearly every home. They are certainly abundant in every school cafeteria! They form the basis for every meal. What are they? Sugared cereals, white bread, pretzels, chips, crackers, cookies, muffins, cakes, candies, white pasta, soda pop, juice drinks, sugary jams and jellies, prepared dinners and "fast" foods. Let's see, is there anything "fun" to eat that I forgot? If so, add it to the list!

These foods provide less fiber, fewer nutrients, and more quick-burning calories. They cause malnutrition (even in affluent societies), lack of energy, sluggish digestion and elimination, and upset the delicate balance of the immune system. What's left to eat? Believe it or not, there are hundreds of delicious, wholesome foods that will put you on the road toward better health.

HOW IMPORTANT IS A HEALTHY IMMUNE SYSTEM?
A malfunctioning immune system is responsible for weight abnormalities, allergies and sensitivities to foods, chemicals, fabrics, dust and pollens, etc., autoimmune diseases such as lupus, Chron's, AIDS, cancers, as well as the common cold, flu, infections, etc.

What CAUSES a weakened immune system? Stress, food additives (including sugar), chemicals, drugs (including alcohol and tobacco) and hidden food allergies are the major culprits in immune system malfunction. Other causes include: over-consumption of cooked foods; excess acid-forming foods such as meats, all dairy products and cooked grains; and all refined foods (white flour, breads, desserts).

ENERGY

What about energy? Is there anyone out there who has enough...or would we all like more? Whole foods are our BEST sources of energy for fueling the body. What IS energy? Calories! What is the best source of calories? Complex carbohydrates.

The body needs calories, but only "good" calories. Not just ANY calories will do, or we could all enjoy excellent health and just store Twinkies, Hershey bars and chocolate kisses. Every body needs the nutrient-dense calories found in wholesome, unrefined fresh fruits, vegetables, nuts, seeds, grains, and legumes.

FIBER

Whole, natural, high-fiber foods can be friend or foe. When switching from refined to whole foods all at once, foods are rushed through the body too quickly for the body to absorb nutrients. This can cause diarrhea, especially when adding the insoluble fiber of grains that travel quickly through the body, cleansing and scouring. Adding the soluble fiber of legumes that travel slowly, absorbing water and adding bulk to the stools, solves the problem!

THE FIBER–CHOLESTEROL CONNECTION

Fiber, most broadly, is the portion of plant foods our bodies can't digest. It comes in two basic categories — insoluble and soluble. Insoluble fibers, which don't dissolve in water, are the more obviously "fibrous" of the two.

These include the woody or structural parts of plants, such as the bran coating around wheat and corn kernels. They pass through the digestive tract largely unchanged and speed the passage of whatever else comes along for the ride.

Soluble fibers, which do dissolve in water, are found in abundance in beans and oats. They have the consistency of a gel and tend to slow the passage of material through the digestive tract. The process of refining foods removes much of the insoluble fiber — hence the widespread NEED for bran and other fiber supplements and laxatives.

Research has shown that cultures that eat only whole foods have no need for extra fiber, nor do those cultures suffer any of the health problems caused from the lack of adequate fiber, such as constipation, colitis, diverticulitis, and colon cancer, to name just a few!

HOW MUCH FIBER IS ENOUGH?
British physician Denis Burkitt found that the rural Africans he studied ate some 50 to 150 grams of fiber a day. Americans, by contrast, typically consume about 20 grams. It is generally accepted by many researchers today that we should double or triple our fiber intake (mainly soluble fibers, eaten as unrefined foods) and cut our fat consumption at least by one half.

To increase soluble fiber intake, we could eat 3 c. of oatmeal per day! Or, how about 1 1/2 c. of oat bran, or 3 standard doses of Metamucil, Fiberall, or other bulk laxatives? One cup of beans provides the same amount of fiber, is much more pleasant to eat and can be served in an endless variety of meals, such as bean dip, bean burritos, or creamy soups.

Since beans are one of the richest sources of fiber and an excellent source of protein with almost no fat, they are one of the best sources of soluble fiber. They also provide a rich source of essential minerals, especially when sprouted.

Increasing fiber foods has the effect of lowering cholesterol - in some cases dramatically. Also important, however, is cutting back on cholesterol-rich foods. This can easily be accomplished by replacing meats with legumes and grains.

PROTEIN

EXCESS PROTEIN CONSUMPTION

Most Americans consume 200% to 400% more protein than needed, resulting in serious health problems. Some of the health abnormalities related to excessive animal protein consumption are: heart disease, arteriosclerosis, premature aging, mental illness, mineral imbalances (causing severe calcium and magnesium deficiencies, as well as deficiencies in vitamins B6 and B3). Sources include the U. S. Army Medical Research and Nutrition Laboratory, Dr. Lennart Krook, and Dr. Uri Nikolayev, as well as doctors from Holland and Denmark.

The National Academy of Science urges us to replace the fattier animal protein with low-fat plant protein, such as whole grains, dried beans, peas, lentils, soybeans and soy products.

According to leading authorities on heart disease, Dr. Dean Ornish, and many others, the body obtains all the amino acids it needs to build protein from plant sources. It is, however, still possible for even strict vegetarians to get too much protein in their diet.

HOW MUCH PROTEIN IS ENOUGH?

Research has shown that any excess protein (from ANY source) is converted into carbohydrates; then, if not burned as energy, it is converted to fat, just as if you ate a huge banana split. Excess protein also puts undue stress on the kidneys and liver, so it is best to rely on foods from the plant kingdom to supply the body's needs. Then monitor closely the protein intake from all sources.

When using concentrated sources of protein, like milk, cheese, tofu, gluten, TVP and protein powders, it is **still** possible to eat too much protein, regardless of the source.

Mother's milk is only about 1 1/2% protein. On this small amount, a baby is able to double its birth weight several times within a few short months. If all that growing and developing takes only a tiny amount of protein, why are we told we need so much more?

George Beinhorn, in Bike World Magazine, states: "The United States Government's own 70-gram recommendation was established on the basis of research that clearly showed 30 grams to be completely adequate. The extra 40 grams were labeled a 'margin of safety.' Though one Food and Nutrition board member reported that the real reason behind the high figure was that the board feared a 'public outcry' over the 30 gram figure."

Eating too much protein at one sitting forces the body to try to process it all at once. Your car's fuel tank can only take so much gasoline. Any excess you try to put in is wasted. If you overfill your body's fuel tank with too much protein (or too much of any fuel), the excess fuel creates harmful toxins that the body must try to process and eliminate.

The body works best with a constant supply of high-quality fuel, so spread out your protein consumption during the day.

HOW MUCH FOOD DOES IT
TAKE TO EQUAL 30 GRAMS OF PROTEIN?

Eating 4 servings per day of grains and 1 serving of legumes provides about 22 grams of good quality protein. A typical day's food choices might include the following: 1 c. brown rice (5g), 1/2 c. black beans (8g), 1 whole wheat pita pocket (6g), and 1/2 c. cracked wheat pilaf (3g).

Fruits and vegetables contain small amounts of protein, usually 1/2g to 1g per serving (potatoes and dark green vegetables provide 3-5g per serving!), making it very easy to get enough protein without adding protein powders or animal proteins.

A little protein powder (1 T = 12g) in a smoothie or a small amount of meat (1 ounce = 6g) or eggs (1 = 6g) eaten as a salad garnish or as an occasional side dish would be acceptable if you cut down on your servings of grain or legumes. But remember, the body needs fiber to move foods quickly through the digestive tract, and it doesn't get ANY fiber from animal proteins.

ANIMAL PROTEIN IS A LOW-QUALITY FUEL

The proteins that make up the human body are NOT obtained directly from the foods we eat. The body must first break down foods into individual amino acids, the "building blocks" of protein. Animal protein, especially beef, the American "protein of choice," is considered a low-quality fuel for humans because there are very strong bonds holding the amino acids together.

This requires that the body expend about half as much energy as that food supplies just to try to liberate the amino acids. The human body is not good at breaking these strong bonds, so the mostly-intact chain of amino acids then becomes toxic because it passes too slowly through the body.

According to Dr. Norman Walker, author of Diet and Salad Suggestions, this process creates a vast amount of uric acid that is absorbed by the muscles where it crystallizes and causes rheumatism, neuritis, sciatica, etc. Thousands of analyses of urine show that without exception, the uric acid present in the urine of meat eaters was far less than what should be eliminated, indicating that the muscles were absorbing from 5 to 10 times what the body should eliminate through the kidneys.

On the other hand, foods from the plant kingdom are easy for the body to use because they contain loosely bound amino acids that are easy for the body to separate and recombine as protein. When you eat a good supply of enzyme-rich plant foods, it doesn't TAKE energy for the body to MAKE energy from plant proteins. The nutrients from plant foods are quickly and easily broken down, then efficiently transported through the body. These are the "high octane" fuels the body needs to run smoothly and efficiently.

COMPLETE AND INCOMPLETE PROTEINS

Plant protein comes from three main classes of foods: legumes (beans, peas and lentils), nuts and seeds, and grains. Proteins from plant sources are "incomplete proteins," because one or more of the eight essential amino acids are missing or in short supply (with the exception of soybeans).

Legumes must be combined with another protein source from another class of foods, such as seeds or grains (or animal products). They are born mixers as well as meat extenders. They can be mixed with grains or meats to stretch your dollar and improve nutrition.

A meal containing legumes and seeds; legumes and grains; or seeds and grains provides all the amino acids needed to supply protein for health and growth. These incomplete proteins can even be eaten as much as 24 hours apart and still combine properly because the body stores the excess amino acids in reserve to be used on an "as needed" basis. When cells need repair, the body can't wait for food to be eaten. It relies on its reserves to supply the necessary amino acids in the right quantities to form the kind of protein necessary for the part of the body needing repair.

FOOD COMBINING FOR PROTEIN COMPLEMENTATION
This makes meal preparation much less complex, allows us to consume meals combined for proper digestion, and lets the body do the work of figuring out what it needs from this meal...and that meal...and the next meal...and so on. As long as we don't "gum up the works" with processed fats, refined flours and sugars, we can count on getting all the protein we need to run our "fine machine."

According to Dr. Lendon Smith, "Eliminating, or drastically reducing meat and dairy products creates a large void in the diet of most Americans. The benefits of using beans on a daily basis have recently been promoted because studies show beans help to reduce cholesterol while providing excellent nutrition. When combined with nuts, seeds or grains, they form a complete high-fiber vegetable protein.

"A three-ounce steak will provide 350 calories and only about 15 grams of usable protein. One and one-fourth cups of cooked beans will provide the same number of calories and yet deliver 50% more usable protein. And, since beans are only 2-3% fat, you have a virtually fat-free source of protein, with NO cholesterol.

"By using beans ground to a flour in all your baked goods, you not only create a perfect protein, you also add valuable B vitamins, carbohydrates and iron. Creamy soups, sauces and gravies to rival canned or packaged brands are thickened with bean flour and made without any fat or dairy products. Busy cooks will be happy to know these soups and sauces cook in only 3 minutes. They're almost instant, much more nutritious, and much less expensive than those available from the supermarket."

COMPLETE PLANT PROTEINS
Gluten (GLOOtun) is made from whole wheat flour and contains the 8 amino acids necessary to make up protein. However, the amino acid lysine in most wheat is low. Adding bean flour in the gluten-making process will add the necessary lysine.

Tofu (TOEfoo) is a complete protein and is made by curdling the milk of soybeans with an acid such as vinegar, ascorbic acid, lemon juice, etc. It is a concentrated protein with a bland flavor that can be seasoned or eaten plain. It makes excellent creamy smoothies and ice cream.

TVP, also a complete protein, is a commercial meat substitute made from soybeans that have been processed at very high temperatures. It is not as easy to digest as gluten and tofu.

COMBINING PLANTS FOR COMPLETE PROTEIN
Properly combining foods from the plant kingdom produces a high quality low-fat protein that is rich in fiber, vitamins and minerals...with NO cholesterol.

High-protein plant foods are divided into three groups, as shown on the chart on the next page. Each category is usually low in one or more amino acids and needs to be combined with foods of another category that are high in that amino acid. The body will then break down these foods into amino acids and store them for up to 24 hours. If foods from corresponding categories are not eaten within that time, the stored amino acids are discarded as waste.

Eating a wide variety of foods ensures that your body will have the right "raw materials" to manufacture a good supply of protein.

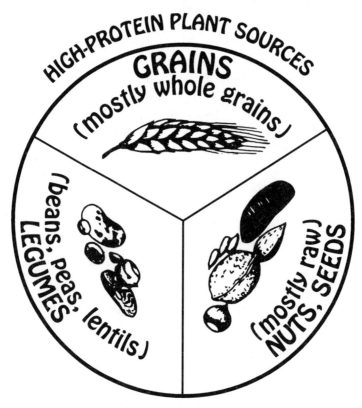

EXAMPLES OF FOODS IN EACH CATEGORY

LEGUMES: Anasazi Beans, Adzuki Beans, Black Lentils, Black Beans, Blackeyed Peas, Fava Beans, Garbanzo Beans, Green Lentils, Green Peas, Kidney Beans, Lima Beans, Mung Beans, Navy Beans, Peanuts, Pink Beans, Pinto Beans, Red Beans, Red Lentils, Scarlet Runner Beans, Small White Beans, Soybeans, Tofu and Soy Products, Yellow Peas

NUTS & SEEDS: Almonds, Brazil Nuts, Cashews, Filberts, Pecans, Flaxseeds, Pumpkin Seeds, Sesame Seeds, Sunflower Seeds, Walnuts

GRAINS: Amaranth, Barley, Buckwheat, Corn, Millet, Oats, Quinoa, Rice, Rye, Spelt, Teff, Triticale, Wheat

COMPARE THE COST

Not only are plant proteins more easily digested and utilized by the body, they are much less expensive. When served as a source of protein, beans cost less than 10¢ per serving, compared to commercial cheeses at 40¢ per serving and meats at a minimum of 75¢ per serving! (Idaho Pea and Lentil Commission)

WHEAT PROTEIN FOR LOW COST MEALS

Gluten is a mixture of proteins found in wheat, and to a smaller degree, in oats, barley and other cereal grains. It helps make dough rise. When separated from the starch and bran in wheat, gluten is an excellent meat substitute. It is high in protein with NO cholesterol and only a trace of fat in each serving. It is much more easily digested than meat, very easy to make into "fake meats," and very inexpensive. LeArta Moulton, in **The Amazing Wheat Book,** gives the following figures:

12 c. whole wheat flour makes 4 c. raw gluten, which bakes into 9 c. ground gluten, which is equivalent to 3 lbs. cooked hamburger!   The wheat flour costs only 56¢ and yields:
>   512 gluten cubes (1/2"x1/2")
>   150 meatballs
>   20 steak slices (4"x1/2")

What's the current cost in your store for 3 lbs. of extra lean hamburger, or extra-lean steaks? (Note: Even if you can *afford* extra-lean hamburger, can you afford the 232 grams of fat, 93 grams of saturated fat, or the 940 milligrams of cholesterol, without ANY fiber, in 3 lbs. of meat? Compare that to only 27 grams of fat, 4 grams of saturated fat, NO cholesterol, and 36 grams of fiber in 3 lbs. of gluten.)

Storing and using whole beans and grains isn't just convenient...it's essential! They are the cheapest foods on earth and no amount of money can buy food that is more nutritious or better utilized by the body. So, STOCK UP!!!

ENZYME SUPPLEMENTS TO STORE

You can purchase enzymes in pill and liquid form that aid in digestion, but there is no perfect substitute for REAL foods, especially raw foods. An enzyme supplement should contain at least three of the essential enzymes: protease, amylase, and lipase, to digest protein, starch, and fat. The missing enzyme, cellulase, breaks down fiber, and since we traditionally eat such small amounts of fiber, this is the one enzyme manufacturers often leave out.

At the time of this writing, the best and only complete, live enzyme supplement source I know of (with all the essential vitamins and minerals) is **Juice Plus+**. Recent research done at Brigham Young University shows that enzymes really DO heal damaged cells in the body, even in people who smoke. Supplementation using this product *strengthens the immune system*, and *repairs DNA*, reducing the incidence of illness and risk of disease. What more could you want? That is all the body needs to build and maintain good health.

For more information on the benefits of this product, or on storing a year's supply of this fine product, call 1-888-232-6706.

STEP 6

FOOD PREPARATION EQUIPMENT

What To Use and How

In preserving and preparing food, many people are fortunate enough to have an ideal combination—a modern kitchen and its appliances, plus equipment used on the farm in grandma's time before "prepared" foods became a way of life.

Cooking with basic beans and grains requires a variety of equipment for grinding, blending and cracking. This is a bonafide case of needing to spend money to save some money. Purchasing good quality equipment is usually a once-in-a-lifetime occurrence. Most good cookware and kitchen equipment is built to last. It helps save money by allowing us to process stored foods at home rather than buying flour, cereals, and other products.

Good equipment also helps save money by supplying the means to preserve and store food to eliminate waste and help us take advantage of perishable food bargains at the market, or of home grown fruits and vegetables which generous neighbors and friends sometimes supply in years of abundant harvest.

TO GRIND GRAIN AND BEANS TO A FLOUR, OR TO COARSELY CRACK FOR QUICKER COOKING:

- ❑ Electric mill
- ❑ Hand grinding mill
- ❑ Electric seed and nut mill (coffee grinder)

ELECTRICAL APPLIANCES:

- ❑ Food blender (mixing non-instant milk, smoothies, chopping nuts and dried fruits, and for grinding grains for "milks")
- ❑ Electric mixer (mixing breads, cakes, cookies, etc.)
- ❑ Champion juicer (juices, ice cream, sno cones, etc.)
- ❑ *Electric bread machine (to bake single loaves)
- ❑ *Food processor (chopping, slicing, mixing)
  (*Optional, but oh so convenient!)

FOR HOME CANNING, FREEZING, DRYING, ETC.:

- ❑ Dehydrator (if you live where you have sufficient produce to dry)
- ❑ Fruit canners/steamers (to process low-acid fruits)
- ❑ Glass jars and sealing lids (I prefer pint and quart sizes)
- ❑ Vegetable steamer (to steam rather than boil vegetables)
- ❑ Freezer bags
- ❑ Pressure cooker - stainless steel (to quickly cook beans, grains, etc.)
- ❑ Pressure canner (to bottle beans, soups, vegetables, meats, etc.)
- ❑ Hand juicer (for citrus fruits)
- ❑ Colander (to drain washed foods, homemade cheeses, etc.)
- ❑ Crocks (for sauerkraut or other salted or pickled foods)
- ❑ Graters (to grate carrots, potatoes, onions, etc. so they cook in only 3 minutes!)

❑ Slicers (to quickly process cabbage, carrots, beans, etc. for cooking, freezing, or pickling)
❑ Vacuum sealer (non-electric, about $20, electric about $150)

MISCELLANEOUS:
❑ Meat grinder (to grind sprouted grains, gluten, nuts and raisins)
❑ Seed sprouting trays (to grow fresh sprouts year-round)
❑ Small and large bread pans
❑ Small and large muffin tins
❑ Small and large cake pans
❑ Baking trays
❑ Strainers
❑ Wire whisks
❑ Ice cream scoop (for measuring meatless patties, cookies, etc.)
❑ Sturdy non-electric can opener (Swing-A-Way)
❑ Pasta maker for pasta, tortillas and pita bread (useful, but not essential)
❑ Heavy-duty cooking pans (stainless steel or cast iron)
❑ Mixing bowls
❑ Cheesecloth or other straining cloths (for making cheeses, tofu, yogurt, etc.)

TO GROW A GARDEN:
❑ Pick, shovel, rake and hoe
❑ Hoses for watering and soaking
❑ Wheelbarrow
❑ String
❑ Hammer or Sledge (to pound stakes...or maybe tough dirt!)

NON-ELECTRIC EQUIPMENT AND SUPPLIES:
An excellent catalog for purchasing non-electric equipment and supplies is Lehman's. Order a copy from P.O. Box 41, Kidron, OH 44636 USA, or call 330-857-5757

You may also contact them by e-mail: getinfo@lehmans.com, or visit their website at http://www.lehmans.com/. The company has been supplying to the Amish and others seeking a simpler and more self-sufficient lifestyle since 1955.

Items in their catalog include hand-powered kitchen appliances, homesteading tools, grain mills, cheese-making supplies, composting toilets, oil lamps and gas lights, water pumps and filters, gas refrigerators, wood-burning stoves, and much more. Many of the items date to the 1800's. They have everything you need to live the kind of life you seek!

STEP 7

THE SWITCH TO WHOLE FOODS

Only one person I know LIKES to spend hours in the kitchen. I don't! I rarely plan far enough ahead to remember the night before to rinse and soak beans and would rather not start 3 hours ahead of mealtime to cook and flavor them. Rarely do I start 1 hour ahead of mealtime to cook whole grains either! How, then, do I make meals in 30 minutes or less?

Spend a little time cooking large batches of whole grains and legumes.
- Freeze cooked grains or beans by placing 2 c. in quart zip-loc bags. Flatten, forcing air out as you go. Stack in freezer. Use within 6 months.
- Dry cooked wheat to make your own Bulgur, whole or cracked. Stores well on the shelf and cooks in only 15 minutes.
- Bottle beans using instructions found on p. 158 of Country Beans, or a current Ball Blue Book.
- Grind grains and beans to a flour so they can be used in baked goods, or cooked in only 3 minutes. Store in refrigerator or freezer if not used within 1 month.
- Crack grains and beans so they will cook in only 15 minutes. Store in refrigerator or freezer if not used within 1 month.
- Make up a few dry mixes - like 5-Minute Bean Dip, 3-Minute Cream Soups or Gravies, 100% Whole Wheat Bread Mix, Pasta, Corn Tortilla, Wheatquick, Seasonings, etc. When you're ready to prepare a meal, you can make it in a FLASH!

PASSPORT TO SURVIVAL RECIPES

Learning to cook with whole foods—whole grains, legumes, nuts and seeds, fruits and vegetables—involves a little more effort than opening a can or a box, but oh what a reward awaits you! Filling, satisfying meals, so low in fat and so high in nutrients, are sure to please the whole family. Don't wait for an emergency to use these recipes. They're perfect for every meal of every day!

GRAINS

Using whole stored grains, you can make a meal in only minutes...*if* you do some advance preparation.
- Keep a supply of cooked grains in the refrigerator or freezer.
- Crack wheat, oats, or rice so they can be on the table or used in a recipe in just 15 minutes, with only 2 minutes of cooking time.
- Grind whole grains and keep the flours fresh by storing them in the refrigerator or freezer, if not used within 1 month.

STEAMED WHEAT OR BROWN RICE

1 c. dry whole kernel wheat   *2 c. water*
1 t. salt

Place ingredients in a 1-2 qt. casserole dish or pan, uncovered, in a larger kettle for steaming (casserole dish set on a canning jar ring or lid, set inside another pan containing about 4 c. additional water and a lid to cover all).

Bring water in bottom of large pan to a full rolling boil; boil about 15 min. Reduce heat and simmer about 6 hours.

OVEN METHOD

Bring all to a boil, then place in a 350° oven for about 4-6 hours. Refrigerate or freeze for storing.

OVERNIGHT THERMOS METHOD

Bring all to a boil, then pour into heated stainless steel or glass-lined thermos bottle. Secure cap. Place bottle on side. In the morning, pour off any additional water, add butter and honey, and serve hot.

PRESSURE COOKER

Place the ingredients listed above into a 4-6 qt. pressure cooker. Secure lid (placing weight on shaft, if your pressure cooker uses one). Bring to a boil over high heat. Reduce heat to medium-low and cook 15 minutes. Bring pressure down by placing pan in sink under a stream of cold water.

Serving suggestions:
Hot, with butter and salt
In place of beans in chili
Mixed with Cream of Mushroom soup as a gravy
As a casserole, with cream soup, celery, onion, bell pepper, etc.
Ground with cheese. Bake until cheese melts.
In place of rice, in casseroles, stir-fry or pilaf

For Cracked Wheat, use 1 cup sifted cracked wheat to 1 3/4 c. water. See Cracked Wheat Cereal recipe in this section.

REFRIGERATING AND FREEZING GRAINS AND BEANS

Cooked grains and beans can be stored in the refrigerator up to 1 week. I like to cook a large batch and fill quart zip-loc bags with 2-cup portions. Flatten bags, forcing out air. Freeze flat, then stack and store in the freezer up to 6 months. I have one stack of a variety of beans, and another of grains. When I want to use them in a recipe, I either break off what I need, or place the package in hot water or the microwave.

BEANS

BEAN FLOURS – FOR *FAST,* HEALTHY MEALS

We all know how long it CAN take to cook beans, but they can now be served as *fast foods* with this breakthrough. *Revolutionary NEW bean soups, from first step to first bite in 3 minutes or less.* So, bring those beans out of the pantry and give them the place on your table they deserve!

Bean flour can be ground at home using an electric or hand grinder. Or purchase flours ground at BOB'S RED MILL, 5209 S. E. INTERNATIONAL WAY, MILWAUKIE, OR 97222, (503) 654-3215. Red Mill products are available in health stores and supermarkets across the U.S., especially on the West Coast. Call for a mail-order catalog or for a retailer near you. Flours available are: White Bean, Black Bean, Pinto Bean, Garbanzo Bean, Green Pea, and Red Lentil.

GRINDING BEAN FLOUR

When added to boiling water, bean flours thicken in only 1 minute, and in 3 minutes are ready to eat. Bean flours added to baked goods increase vitamins and minerals and provide a source of complete protein.

Modern equipment for the kitchen has revolutionized the use of beans! Dry beans can be ground to a fine flour using a hand grinder for small quantities, or electric mills for larger quantities. Bean flour stores for up to 6 months on the shelf, 1 year under refrigeration, is great to have on hand for "instant" soups, sauces, dips, sandwich fillings and gravies, and to add to almost everything you cook or bake.

Baby lima and small white beans are my favorite because they can be used to make great cream sauces and soups which are gluten-free, wheat-free, fat-free and dairy-free. Also, the flours can be added to any recipe calling for wheat flour to achieve protein complimentation and to add additional fiber and essential nutrients. Other favorites are pinto, small red and garbanzo.

There are at least 2 electric home mills which are guaranteed to grind all types of grains and beans to a flour as fine as wheat flour. These are the K-TEC Kitchen Mill, and the GrainMaster Whisper Mill. The Back To Basics hand mill will also grind grains and beans to a flour, although not quite as fine. All of these mills can be ordered by calling 1-888-232-6706. Mills with *grinding stones* must be cleaned after each 2 cups of beans by grinding 1 cup of hard wheat. Do not grind soy beans if your mill uses grinding stones. If beans are too large to go easily into the grinding chamber of your electric mill, crack first with a blender or hand grain cracker.

Sort beans, checking for broken, dirty beans or rock pieces. (Most beans nowdays have been "triple cleaned," making this step unnecessary.) Pour into hopper of your mill. I like to place the mill in my kitchen sink to eliminate most of the bean dust from grinding. Set mill to grind on medium-fine. The resulting flour should be as fine as the wheat flour used in baking breads, cookies, etc. (A small electric seed or coffee mill, or heavy-duty blender can be used, but will produce a more coarse flour.)

Turn on mill and begin stirring beans (if necessary) where they go into the grinding chamber (with the handle of a spoon) so they will not get stuck. This is not necessary in some mills, or when grinding smaller beans, peas and lentils. The sponge filter should be cleaned after each 2 cups of beans in the K-TEC. (Or, keep an extra filter on hand.) If bean dust is being thrown from mill, cover mill with a large kitchen towel, leaving only a small opening for stirring beans.

Beans which have absorbed excess moisture will cause caking on electric mill parts. Thoroughly brush away flour residue from mill after each use. (I like to use a clean, stiff paint brush.) If using a mill with grinding stones, run 1 cup of dry grain through the mill to clean out internal parts, then clean as instructed above. Store flour in an air tight container, preferably in the refrigerator if not used within several weeks.

3-MINUTE BEAN FLOUR SOUPS

Use 2 T. white bean flour per cup of liquid for thin soups or just to add flavor and color, 3 T. for medium-thick and 4-5 T. for thick soups, stews or gravies. Whisk into soup stock, or use hot water flavored with 1 t. meat-based or vegetable soup base per cup of water. Cook and stir 3 minutes. Blend after cooking, if desired, for a creamier soup. For pea and lentil soups, use only 1 T. flour per cup of liquid for thin soups, 2 T. for medium and 3 T. for thick soups.

My favorite is a "cup-a-soup" using 1 c. cool water, 1 chicken or vegetable bouillon cube and 1 T. any variety of pea or lentil flour. Mix and heat to boiling; reduce heat to medium-low; cover pan and simmer 2 minutes.

To thicken already-cooked soups containing vegetables, noodles, etc.: For 6 c. soup, blend 1/2 to 1 c. bean flour (depending on how thick and creamy you want the soup to be) and 2 c. cooled soup broth on high speed for 1 minute. Whisk into hot soup mixture and cook 4-5 minutes over medium high heat, stirring occasionally. Note: Blending is not essential, but produces a creamier texture.

CREAMY BLENDER SOUPS WITHOUT A GRINDER!

For Pea or Lentil Soup, cook 3/4 c. dry peas or lentils in 6 c. boiling water for 10 minutes. Blend 2 minutes on high. Return to pan; add 2 T. chicken bouillon or soup base, and cook an additional 3 minutes.

For Creamy White Bean Soup, cook 1 c. dry white beans in 3 c. boiling water for 20 minutes. Drain and rinse. Blend approximately 1 c. beans at a time with 2 c. hot water on high speed (8 c. water total). Repeat until all beans are blended, straining out any large pieces.

Return to saucepan adding 2 T. chicken or vegetable soup base and salt and pepper to taste. Cook 5 minutes over medium heat. Use as cream soup or as a creamy soup base, adding fresh veggies in season.

TRADITIONAL METHODS FOR COOKING BEANS

SOAKING DRY BEANS

Dry beans, whole peas, and split peas (unless used in soup) need soaking before cooking. Lentils do not.

• Overnight soak: Wash and sort beans; place in large sauce pan with 6 cups of water per pound of beans. Let stand overnight.

• Quick soak: Follow above instructions, but bring beans and water to a boil and cook 2 minutes. Remove from heat, cover, let stand 1 hour.

• Cracked bean Quick soak: To 2 c. of beans that have been coarsely cracked using a hand grain cracker, blender, or small coffee grinder, add 4 cups boiling water. Cover and let stand 5 minutes; rinse (in strainer) and drain.

Whole, soaked beans can be cooked in a variety of ways, or frozen to speed cooking time even further. Cook soaked beans slowly over low heat to prevent broken or floating skins. A tablespoon of oil or butter added during cooking reduces foaming and boil-overs.

COOKING TIMES

These times are approximate. They differ according to altitude, age and moisture content of beans, and soaking method. The following list is a fairly complete list of average cooking times for soaked beans:

Black beans - 1 to 1 1/2 hrs.
Black-eyed peas - 1 to 1 1/2 hr.
Garbanzo beans - 2 to 2 1/2 hr.
Great Northern beans - 1 to 1 1/2 hrs.
Kidney beans - 1 1/2 to 2 hrs.
Lentils - 30-45 min. (NO soaking required.)
Limas, baby - 1 to 1 1/2 hrs.
Pink, pinto and red beans - 1 1/2 to 2 hrs.
Soybeans - 3 to 3 1/2 hrs.
Split peas, green and yellow - 35 to 45 min. (NO soaking required.)
White beans (navy) small - 1 to 1 1/2 hrs.

Note: Old beans ground to a flour still cook in only 3 minutes for soups. If using very old beans, make a small amount of soup to test for bitter flavor before using in soups or breads, etc.

COOKING CRACKED BEANS
Place soaked cracked beans in saucepan with hot water to cover. Bring to a boil; cover pan, then turn heat to medium-low and cook for 15-25 minutes, depending on texture desired (firm for stir fry or to mix with cracked wheat or pilaf, soft for creamy soups, casseroles or loaves).
• Cracked soaked beans are excellent to add to stir fry. Cook in a small amount of oil until lightly browned.
• Add soaked, drained cracked beans to soups and cook for 20-30 min.
• Cook soaked, drained cracked beans with equal parts rice for pilaf.

COOKING LENTILS
To cook lentils, combine 2 c. lentils and 5 c. water in a saucepan. Bring to boiling, reduce heat, cover tightly, and boil gently for 30 minutes. Lentils do not require pre-soaking. Cook sprouted lentils only 5-10 min.

COOKING BEANS IN A CROCK POT
Place washed and sorted beans in boiling water (enough to cover) and simmer for 10 minutes. Drain off water. Then place beans in crockery cooker and add 6 cups of water per pound of beans and add seasonings to taste. Cook on low 12 hrs.

COOKING BEANS IN A PRESSURE COOKER
Soak washed and sorted beans by either the overnight or quick method. Drain and rinse. Place in pressure cooker (cooker should be no more than 1/3 filled to allow for expansion). Add water to cover and 1 T. of oil to reduce foaming.

Cover; cook at 10 pounds pressure 10-20 minutes, depending on size of bean. OR, place washed and sorted beans - unsoaked - in pressure cooker with 3 times as much water as beans and 2-3 teaspoons of oil or butter. Cover; cook at 15 pounds pressure for 30 minutes for small beans, 40 minutes for large beans. Variance in time is due to the inherent texture of each different variety of bean.

For more information and nearly 400 bean recipes (with over 120 FAST bean flour recipes!), see my book, **Country Beans**.

WHAT TO EAT
WHEN YOU'RE OUT OF MEAT

Gluten (GLOOtun) is a meat substitute that can be made at home from whole wheat flour and contains the 8 amino acids necessary to make a complete protein. However, the amino acid lysine in most wheat is low. Adding bean flour in the gluten-making process will add the necessary lysine.

Used in various main dish recipes gluten makes emergency meals more appetizing. It doesn't take long to learn how to make it, and then comes the fun of experimenting with recipes, trying to make it taste more like meat. If meat and cheese are scarce, use them in very small amounts as flavoring for gluten dishes.

GLUTEN
(Protein Part of Wheat)
bowl of 10 c. flour   *lukewarm water (6-8 cups)*

Stir while adding enough water to moisten flour. (See the **Quick Wholesome Foods** video for texture.) Let rest 1/2 hour or more, then add a small amount of clear water to the bowl. Work and squeeze with your hands to loosen the dough (less than a minute). When the water takes on a milky appearance and you see specks of bran, pour this water off, holding bulk of the dough back with your hands. Over a sink, place this cough in a colander (plastic works best) with another bowl placed underneath the colander to catch any of the gluten that slips through the holes. Under a tap of slowly running lukewarm water, work and squeeze the dough with your hands until the gluten starts to hold together and the liquid coming from the dough is clear. It is not necessary to rinse out all of the bran from the gluten. In about 3-5 minutes, you should have a ball of elastic-like dough. This is Raw Gluten.

Raw Gluten can now be cooked using any of the following methods:

- Vegetable steamer - 30 minutes, or until firm
- Double boiler - 30 minutes, or until firm
- Pressure cooker - 15 minutes at 15 lb. pressure (with or without broth seasoning)
- Cut cooked, firm gluten into slices (for steaks or chipped "beef"); strips (for stir-fry or gravies); cubes (for chicken dishes); or grind (for "hamburger" or candy recipes).

FLAVORING THE GLUTEN
Simmer unflavored cut gluten (not the ground texture) 3-5 minutes in 1/4" to 1/2" seasoned broth (beef, chicken, ham, crab or herb seasoning mixes).

PREPARING THE GLUTEN
Bread and pan-fry the steaks, top with sauce. Just before serving, add cubes to soups, gravies, seafood dishes; include strips in stir-fry and use for jerky. Season ground gluten and add to chili, taco sauce, pizza, etc. just before serving. See **The Amazing Wheat Book** by LeArta Moulton for detailed instructions and seasoning suggestions.

3-MINUTE TOFU
6 c. hot water   *2 c. fine soy flour*

Coat heavy saucepan with baking spray and heat until oil browns slightly. Add water and bring to a boil, then whisk in soy flour. Bring to a full boil over high heat (be careful, because it boils over easily), stirring constantly (about 30 seconds). VERY gently, stir in 3 T. white vinegar or fresh lemon juice to form curds and clear liquid. Pour into cheesecloth. Rinse gently under cool running water. Gather edges of cloth together and twist to squeeze out as much whey as possible. Squeeze out excess liquid with your hands. The harder you squeeze, the firmer the tofu.

Use in patties, meat loaf, scrambled with eggs, etc. May be eaten plain, seasoned with salt and pepper, or seasoning of your choice, such as taco. Because this tofu retains all the fiber of the soybean, it is softer than the following recipe.

5-MINUTE TOFU
6 c. hot water   *2 c. fine soy flour*

Coat heavy saucepan with baking spray and heat until oil browns slightly. Add water and bring to a boil, then whisk in soy flour. Bring to a full boil over high heat (be careful, because it boils over easily), stirring constantly (about 30 seconds). Pour into cheesecloth-lined strainer (4 layers, about 15" square) set in a large bowl to gather milk. To strain, gather the four edges of the cheesecloth, twist together, and use a spoon or spatula to press mixture down from the twisted part to a ball at the bottom. Press out as much milk as possible. Rinse cheesecloth, and use it to line colander again.

Pour milk back into pan. Reheat milk just until it begins to boil. Remove from heat. VERY gently, stir in 3 T. white vinegar or fresh lemon juice to form curds and clear liquid. Place pan back on burner and cook another 30 seconds. Pour into cheesecloth. Rinse gently in cool water. Gather edges of cloth together and twist to squeeze out as much whey as possible. Place under cool running water and squeeze out excess liquid with your hands. The harder you squeeze, the firmer the tofu.

Use lightly pressed tofu in shakes, patties, meat loaf, scrambled with eggs, etc. May be eaten plain, seasoned with salt and pepper, or seasoning of your choice.

"Meat"balls - Mix 1 c. firm curds, 1 T. pinto bean flour, 1 egg, 2 t. dry minced onion, 1 T. beef bouillon, pepper to taste and 1 c. cooked brown rice. Shape into balls or burgers and brown in a skillet coated with cooking spray.

Taco "Meat" - Place firm curds in a small mixing bowl. Add 2 T. wheat or rice flour and season with 2 T. taco seasoning mix, or to taste. Cook to firm in a heavy skillet, stirring with a fork to keep curds separated. May be seasoned to taste like chicken, beef, etc. May be shaped into patties and browned in a skillet coated with cooking spray, or baked at 350° for 20 minutes.

For sliced **"Tofu Overs,"** flatten ball slightly, then open cheesecloth and cut into strips (or form into patties before pressing). Season with salt, pepper, or other seasoning mix. I like to add a little soy sauce and a drop or two of sesame oil. Brown in heavy skillet coated with baking spray. Start on medium-high and brown on one side. Turn to low, cover pan, and brown on other side.

TRADITIONAL TOFU

Using the instructions and "quick" 30-minute method found on page 152-153 of **Country Beans,** you can make a large batch of tofu in less than 30 minutes. This complete protein food is excellent as a base for patties and meatless loaves, and can be served (and hidden) in hundreds of different ways.

CONVENIENCE FOODS

You can make your own quick mixes for virtually any flour product that can be purchased in the grocery store, at a fraction of the cost and store them in only a fraction of the space. My favorites mixes are *cream soups, pancakes, pasta,* and *bean dips.*

SOUPS

Cream soups made from bean flours cook in only 3 minutes! Four tablespoons white bean flour and 2 teaspoons chicken bouillon combine to make a creamy substitute equal to a whole can of store-bought cream soup, taking up only 1/4 as much storage space. A microwaveable container of instant soup purchased from the grocery store takes up 8 to 10 times as much space as bean flour and seasonings. (Choose a good-quality chicken bouillon made without MSG, or use vegetable bouillon.)

INSTANT CREAM OF CHICKEN SOUP MIX

1 c. white bean flour

2 T. chicken bouillon granules or 6 bouillon cubes, blended to a powder

Combine and place in glass or plastic container. Store up to one month on the shelf, indefinitely if refrigerated or frozen. Makes 6 servings. To make **Soup For Two**, whisk **4 1/2 T. mixture** into **2 c. hot water**. Bring to a boil, then reduce heat and cook an additional 2 minutes. If desired, add 1 c. cooked vegetables and/or pasta; heat through.

CREAMY INSTANT LENTIL SOUP MIX

1 c. red lentil flour

1/4 c. chicken bouillon granules or 12 bouillon cubes, blended to a powder

Combine and place in glass or plastic container. Store up to one month on the shelf, indefinitely if refrigerated or frozen. Makes 12 servings. To make **Soup For Two**, whisk **3 1/2 T. mixture** into **2 c. hot water**. Bring to a boil, then reduce heat and cook an additional 2 minutes. If desired, add 1 c. cooked vegetables and/or pasta; heat through.

BEAN DIPS

Commercially packaged "instant" refried beans are extra-fluffy, requiring more than four times as much space as the bean flour and seasonings in my 5-Minute Refried Bean Dip, and both options take the same amount of time to prepare! To make a meal in a flash, spread flour tortillas with bean dip, fat-free cottage cheese, and salsa. Bake or microwave until heated through. Serve topped with shredded lettuce, chopped tomatoes and onions, and sprinkle with chopped olives.

5-MINUTE REFRIED BEAN DIP

3 c. pinto or black bean flour 1 t. cumin
1 T. chili powder   1 T. salt
1/4 t. garlic powder   2 t. instant minced onions (opt.)

Mix and store in airtight container. Store up to one month on the shelf, indefinitely if refrigerated. To prepare, whisk 3/4 c. of mixture into 2 1/2 c. boiling water. Cook, while stirring, over medium heat for about 1 minute, until mixture thickens. Reduce heat to low. Cover pan and cook 4 minutes. Add 1/2 c. Picante sauce (or to taste). Mixture thickens as it cools and will stay thick even after reheating.

QUICK BREADS

Pancake mixes and *Wheatquick* are easy to prepare and take up very little storage space. Mixes purchased in the store are usually mostly box, requiring about a third more storage space as a homemade mix. (See p. 56 of **Natural Meals** for Wheatquick recipe.)

HIGH PROTEIN PANCAKE/WAFFLE MIX

10 c. fine whole wheat flour   *2 t. baking soda*
2 c. fine white bean flour   *1 1/2 t. salt*
1/4 c. baking powder   *2 c. dry milk powder*

Mix and store in airtight container. Store up to one month on the shelf, indefinitely if refrigerated. To prepare pancakes for 4, add **2 1/4 c. of** *above mixture* to the following:

2 c. warm water   *1 T. honey*
1 1/2 T. olive oil or 3 T. applesauce 2 beaten eggs or substitute

For extra crunch and protein, add 1/4 c. nuts or sunflower seeds to batter.

PASTA

Consider the amount of storage space required for *spaghetti* and *egg noodles*. One cup of flour and salt makes enough noodles to fill a quart jar...occupying only one fourth as much space! It takes only about 5 minutes to combine ingredients, roll and cut the dough into strips. It doesn't even take any special equipment. I have a pasta maker, but find it faster to roll and cut noodles by hand than to use and clean the machine. Pasta does not need to be dried. Just drop into boiling water or soup and cook about 5 minutes, depending on thickness of the dough.

You can add a variety of seasonings, such as oregano, basil, or dry parmesan cheese. For vegetable pasta, add pureed tomatoes, carrots, potatoes, etc. in place of part of the water (or dried, powdered vegetables in place of part of the flour). These cooked pastas make an excellent side dish, served with fresh vegetables.

Most recipes call for a whole egg. My family can't tell the difference in pasta made without the egg, so I most often use just flour, water, and seasonings.

BASIC PASTA

6 c. whole wheat flour   *1 1/2 tsp. salt*
1/2 c. white bean flour
To make pasta for 2 or noodle soup for 6, place 1 c. + 1 T. dry ingredients in a small mixing bowl. Make a well in the center. Place **3 T. water, or 1 egg** in the center and mix to form a stiff dough that barely holds together. If too dry, add water, 1/2 t. at a time.

Sprinkle a bread board lightly with flour and knead the dough on the board for 2 minutes. Roll out 1/8" to 1/16" thick, and cut in strips 1/4" to 1" wide, depending on how wide you like your noodles. (I like to use a pizza cutter.) Or, cut into squares or other fancy shapes; use pinking shears or a notched roller knife.

Drop noodles, a few at a time, into 6 c. boiling water with 1 t. salt added (opt.). Boil about 5 minutes, or until tender. Cooking time will depend on thickness of noodles.

SPINACH PASTA
Add to Basic Pasta recipe:
2 T. spinach, chopped very fine

HERB PASTA
Add to Basic Pasta recipe:
2 T. minced strong herbs (sage, rosemary, thyme, oregano, or marjoram)

PIE CRUST

You can toss almost any grains, beans and vegetables into a soup and create a nutritious meal. You can do the same with a pie crust. Whether you top your ingredients with another crust, mashed potatoes, cracker or bread crumbs, you can still get away with hiding a lot of nutritious ingredients inside.

To avoid the trans-fatty acids in shortening and the cholesterol in butter and lard, I use vegetable oil in my crust, preferably olive oil.

WHOLE WHEAT PIE CRUST MIX
6 c. whole wheat flour　　　　　1 1/2-2 c. vegetable oil
1 T. salt

Mix flour and salt. Gradually add vegetable oil, stirring well, or use electric mixer. If not used within 1 month, store in refrigerator or freezer. *(More oil makes the crust more tender, but I'd rather have fewer calories.)*

To make a double crust, measure 2 1/8 c. dry mix. Sprinkle 6-8 t. ice water on mixture, stirring lightly with a fork. Do not overmix.

Shape into a ball and place half of ball in a gallon zip-loc or large plastic bag (the kind you get at the grocery store when you buy fruits and vegetables). Roll out to fit pan. Cut sides of bag and peel off one side of plastic. Lay exposed crust on pan. Remove other side of plastic and press crust into pan. Repeat with top crust.

If single crusts start to get too brown during baking, cut thin strips of aluminum foil and cover crust, pressing excess foil under rim of pie pan.

BASIC POT PIE

With bottom crust in place, layer cooked, sliced *potatoes*, lightly steamed chopped *celery, onions, carrots* and *peas* to fill pan. Add 1 c. cooked meat, if desired. Cover with *2 cups 3-minute Cream Of Chicken Soup* or other cream sauce or gravy. Add top crust. Pinch edges to seal. Cut shapes or slits in crust and bake at 350° for 30 minutes. Serve with additional cream sauce.

GRAIN "MILKS"

Non-dairy "milk" from grains is excellent for those with milk allergies, strict vegetarians, and as a way of using more stored grains. Other "milk" recipes made from grains, nuts and seeds, are available in my book, **1-2-3 Smoothies.**

RICE MILK

1/2 c. brown rice   *2 t. honey*
2 c. water   *1 t. vanilla*

Place dry rice in a blender, grain mill or seed mill; grind to a powder. Combine with remaining ingredients. Blend 2 minutes, then strain. Add a dash of salt, if desired. Makes 2 cups. Use within 3 days.

Note: To save time, I like to grind and refrigerate quarts of rice and other grains to use in making milks, such as barley and oats.

POWDERED MILK CHEESES

Cottage cheese in 3 minutes? Firm curds (excellent for dips and sandwich spreads) can be made quickly and easily with a minimum of equipment. Add buttermilk and salt to flavor.

SOFT COTTAGE CHEESE

2 c. hot water   *1 1/2 c. dry milk powder*
3 T. fresh lemon juice or white vinegar

Blend water and dry milk and pour into saucepan coated with non-stick cooking spray (foam and all). Sprinkle lemon juice and vinegar slowly around edges and gently stir over medium heat just until milk begins to curdle, separating into curds and whey. Remove from heat and let rest 1 minute. Pour into a strainer or colander, rinse with hot then cold water. Press out water with back of spoon. Makes about 1 1/2 c. curds. If desired, moisten rinsed curds with a little buttermilk before serving. Add salt to taste.

PARMESAN CHEESE

1 c. hot water   *1 c. dry milk powder*
3 T. reconstituted lemon juice

Blend all ingredients and pour into saucepan coated with non-stick cooking spray (foam and all). Cook over medium-high heat until milk boils. Curds will be very small and milk will be frothy. Pour into a cloth-lined strainer, rinse and press out excess water. Put curds into a bowl and stir with a fork to break up. Spread on a baking sheet and dry about 10 minutes in a 150° oven. This cheese can be lightly salted and mixed with 1/4 c. commercial dried Parmesan. Refrigerate. Flavor improves even more as cheese ages.

For many more almost instant cheeses, yogurt, buttermilk, cream cheese, and other powdered milk recipes, see Natural Meals In Minutes, p. 114.

Ready, set? Let's get cookin!
BREAKFASTS

STEAMED WHEAT

For plump, fluffy, separate grains, cook by surrounding the kernels with live steam. This takes a combination of pans, one inside the other. Cook plenty of wheat and keep it refrigerated to use all week long.

5 c. wheat	*canning jar ring or other support*
7 c. water	*small open pan or casserole*
1 T. salt	*larger pan*

Put ingredients in the small pan (or casserole) and set it on the rack in the larger pan. Pour water in the large pan to within 1" of the bottom of the small pan. Cover large pan and turn heat to high. After 15 minutes, reduce heat to medium and steam 4 hours. To bake in the oven, combine 5 c. wheat with 10 c. boiling water and place pan in 350° oven for 3-4 hours. Excellent as a breakfast cereal, in sandwich fillings, ground and flavored for snacks, mixed with ground meats as an extender, etc.

ROLLED WHEAT: Roll cooked wheat thin using a rolling pin. Bake at 350° until partially dried out. Serve hot or cold.

RAW WHEAT PANCAKES

For those without a grinder...

1 c. wheat kernels	*2 t. baking powder*
1 T. olive oil (opt.)	*1/2 t. salt*
2 eggs, separated	*2 T. dry milk powder*

Soak 1 c. whole wheat kernels overnight in 2 cups water. Drain, reserving 3/4 cup liquid. Beat whites separately. Add soaked wheat and reserved liquid to blender. Process on high until very smooth, about 2 minutes. Add egg yolks and dry ingredients. Pour batter into mixing bowl and fold in egg whites. Ladle onto hot griddle and cook until browned on both sides.

113

FLUFFY BUTTERMILK PANCAKES

2 c. fine whole wheat flour
1/4 t. salt (optional)
1/4 c. dry milk powder
1 T. baking powder
1 3/4 c. warm water

1/2 c. buttermilk
1 T. honey
1 t. vanilla
2 T. applesauce or canola oil
4 egg whites, beaten stiff*

Stir dry ingredients well. Make a little "nest" in the flour mixture and add moist ingredients (except egg whites), stirring only until flour is moistened so the pan- cakes will be tender and light. Fold egg whites into batter. Ladle onto hot griddle or waffle iron and cook until brown on both sides. Try adding 1/2 t. ginger or allspice for variety. Serves 4 hungry kids.
*Note: if oil is added, use only 2 egg whites.

CREAMY WHEAT CEREAL

2/3 c. farina*   3 1/4 c. hot water
1/4 c. dry milk powder (opt.)

*Farina is very finely cracked grain, usually rice or wheat. When I sift cracked grains, I end up with 3 products: coarse cracked grain; farina, coarse flour. I use the coarse cracked grain for cereals, salads, sandwich fillings and pilaf. I add the coarse flour to breads and use the farina for creamy cereals, or in breads and muffins.

Microwave: Stir all ingredients in a 6-cup microwave bowl. Cook on high for 1 minute. Stir well. Cook 2-3 minutes more until cereal thickens, stirring every 30 seconds. Stir. Let stand to desired consistency.

Stovetop: Heat water to boiling. Gradually stir in combined farina and milk (if used). Cook 2 minutes, stirring occasionally. Remove from heat and cover. Let stand 2 minutes before serving. Season with honey or maple syrup. Serve with milk or milk substitute. Serves 4.

HONEY MAPLE GRANOLA

7 c. rolled oats   1 c. chopped nuts
1 c. whole wheat flour   1 c. coconut
1/2 c. olive oil   1 T. ground sunflower seeds
1 c. honey, melted   1 T. ground flax seeds
2 t. ea. vanilla and maple extracts   grated rind of one lemon

Mix dry ingredients, then add honey, water or oil, vanilla and mapleine. Mix well and spread out on baking sheets. Bake 2 hours at 150°F, stirring every half hour. Add 2 cups raisins or chopped dates after baking, if desired. Makes about 1 gallon.

Note: Adding seeds and nuts increases the fat content, but growing children and active adults need more fat and the nutrients these foods provide. You may also substitute apple juice concentrate for the canola oil.

CRACKED WHEAT OR RICE CEREAL

1 3/4 c. water   1 c. cracked wheat

Wheat or rice can be cracked at home in a blender, seed mill, or hand grain mill. Sift to remove the flour and very fine grain particles.

Put water and grain into a heavy saucepan. Bring to a FULL boil. Cover, turn off heat and let set 15 minutes, or until water is absorbed. Serve hot with milk and honey. Serves 4.

To save for use in other recipes, such as sandwich fillings, patties, and casseroles, package cooked grains in 2-cup portions in quart zip-loc bags. Flatten to force out air. Stack flat and freeze for up to 3 months.

BREAKFAST STRIPS: Press 2 c. cooked cereal mixed with 2 t. chicken bouillon into a baking dish and chill. Cut into 1" x 3" strips. Toast on all sides under broiler. Serve plain or with gravy or catsup or salsa.

BULGAR WHEAT: Spread 4 c. cooked wheat on baking sheets and dry in 200° oven until crunchy. Stores unrefrigerated for several months. To use, combine 1 c. dry bulgar with 1 1/2 c. water. Bring to a boil. Turn off heat. Let rest 15 minutes. Use in any recipe calling for cooked wheat or rice.

TOASTUM DRINK

4 T. Toastum Crystals   5 c. water

For those who like a hot beverage for breakfast, this drink hits the spot. Parch dry whole wheat, brown rice, barley, or garbanzo beans (or a combination of all of them) until dark brown in a skillet or on a tray in a 350° oven. Crush fine in a blender, seed mill, hand grain mill, or with a hammer. Store Toastum Crystals in an air-tight container. To serve: In a small saucepan or tea kettle, bring water to a boil. Add crystals and turn heat to low. Simmer 5 minutes, strain and serve. Excellent served with evaporated milk (homemade, of course!), honey, vanilla, and nutmeg.

QUICK BEAN SOUPS

These quick soups are excellent for a quick meal or snack. They can also serve as a base for almost any soup or casserole. Just add cooked vegetables (peas, carrots, corn, potatoes, onions, celery, etc.) to the completed soups for a hearty meal. Cooked beans and grains may also be added.

3-MINUTE "CREAM OF CHICKEN" SOUP

This "practically perfect" substitute for canned Cream of Chicken soup is made without milk or fat, so can be used freely on any weight reduction diet.

6 c. boiling water   2 T. chicken or vegetable soup base
1 c. fine white bean flour*   *1 c. diced chicken pieces (opt.)*

*I like small white or navy beans best.

In a medium saucepan over medium heat, whisk bean flour into boiling water and add base. Stir and cook 3 minutes. Blend for 1-2 minutes. Add chicken, if used. Serves 3-4.

RITA'S LENTIL SOUP

4 c. hot water   2 t. lentil soup seasoning
4 T. lentil flour

In a medium saucepan over medium heat, whisk bean flour into boiling water and add base. Stir and cook 3 minutes. Serves 3-4.

RITA'S LENTIL SOUP SEASONING

10 T. salt   2 1/2 t. garlic powder
3 T. black pepper   7 T. parsley flakes
3 T. onion powder   3 T. paprika

Combine and store in air-tight container. Can also be used to season patties, loaves, casseroles and toppings.

INSTANT PEA SOUP

2 c. boiling water   2 t. chicken or vegetable bouillon
3 T. pea flour - green or yellow

In a medium saucepan over medium heat, whisk bean flour into boiling water and bouillon. Stir and cook 3 minutes. Serves 3-4.

BREADS

CINNAMON-RAISIN MUFFINS

1/3 c. honey
2/3 c. orange juice
1 c. raisins
3 T. lemon juice
2 ripe bananas, mashed
1/3 c. applesauce or canola oil

2 c. whole wheat flour
1 t. baking powder
1 t. baking soda
1/2 t. salt
1 1/2 t. cinnamon

In a small saucepan, bring honey, orange juice and raisins to a boil. Remove from heat and let cool while assembling other ingredients. Combine all moist ingredients. Using electric mixer, beat well. Add remaining ingredients and beat until smooth. Coat 6 muffin tins with cooking spray and fill 3/4 full. Bake at 350°F 25 minutes.

EMERGENCY HONEY FROSTING

1/2 c. honey
1/2 t. vanilla or other flavoring

1/2 c. dry milk powder

Bring honey to a boil. Put in top of double boiler. Add dry milk and continue cooking, beating frosting with electric mixer until fluffy. Spread on warm muffins. Frosting sets up when cool.

BANANA SPICE MUFFINS

2 ripe bananas, mashed
1/3 c. honey
2/3 c. orange juice
3 T. lemon juice
1/3 c. applesauce or canola oil

2 c. whole wheat flour
1 t. baking powder
1 t. baking soda
1/2 t. salt
1 t. powdered allspice

Using electric mixer, beat moist ingredients. Add remaining ingredients and beat until smooth. Fill muffin tins, coated with cooking spray, 3/4 full. Bake at 350°F 25 minutes.

100% WHOLE WHEAT BREAD

(REGULAR AND BREAD MACHINE)

1 1/3 c. water   *3 2/3 c. whole wheat flour*
4 T. applesauce (or oil)   *1 1/2 T. dry milk powder*
3 T. honey (or sugar)   *3 T. vital wheat gluten*
1 1/2 t. salt   *2 1/2 t. active dry yeast*

For bread machine, measure all ingredients except yeast into 1 1/2 lb. baking pan in the order listed above. Add yeast last, ensuring that it does not touch any liquids. Select WHOLE GRAIN option. Remove from pan and let cool before storing in plastic bag.

To bake in a conventional oven, combine all ingredients except for 1 cup flour. Stir hard about 1 minute. Add remaining flour, as needed and knead well. Dough should be smooth--not too floury, not too sticky. Form a ball and let rest 5 minutes. Knead well on oiled surface and let rise until double, about 1 hour. (OR Micro-rise using level 2-3 or Low on your microwave... Place donut-shaped ball of dough in glass mixing bowl; cover with plastic wrap and place in microwave along with a glass of cool water. Heat for 3 minutes. Let rest 6 minutes. Heat another 3 minutes. Dough is now ready to shape.) Knead well and form into two leaves. Let rise until doubled, about 1 hour. Bake at 450°F for 15 minutes, then 350°F 25-30 minutes, or until loaf sounds hollow when tapped. Turn onto a rack to cool. Store in airtight plastic bag.

BREAD STICKS

On a bread board, roll out dough 1/2" thick. Cut with round lid or cookie cutter. Cut each piece in half and roll each piece into a long "snake." Dip in egg yolk or evaporated milk, and roll in sesame seeds. Allow to rise until dough doubles in bulk, then bake at 400°F until brown and crisp. Makes about 25 bread sticks.

WHOLE WHEAT FLOUR TORTILLAS

2 c. fine whole wheat flour   1/2 t. salt
1 1/4 t. baking powder   1 T. canola oil
3/4 c. water

Mix all together in a 2-qt. bowl. Knead about 5 minutes, until elastic. Let rest 15 minutes, then cut dough into 10 equal portions.

Roll each into a ball, then roll out on floured surface until very thin and round. Brown on both sides in an ungreased skillet over medium-high heat. Makes 10 tortillas.

CORN TORTILLAS

1 c. boiling water   1/4 c. fine whole wheat flour
2 t. chicken-flavored bouillon   3/4 c. cornmeal
2 t. olive oil   1 T. buttermilk or water

Add bouillon and oil to boiling water, then stir in flour and cornmeal until well mixed. Mix in buttermilk. Shape into 1" balls, then place each on a floured surface and roll into 6" circles. Cook in a hot, ungreased skillet until the edges are crisp and brown. Or, cook only until firm and slightly browned, then turn over, add filling of your choice and roll. Corn tortillas are delicious served plain, buttered, or with a variety of toppings or fillings. Makes 12.

KRISTY'S CORNBREAD

1 c. fine cornmeal   1/4 t. salt
1 c. flour   1 c. buttermilk
1/3 c. honey   1/4 c. oil
2 1/2 t. baking powder   1 large egg or 1 T. vinegar

Preheat oven to 400°F. Grease 8" square pan. Combine dry ingredients. Stir in buttermilk, oil and egg. Pour into pan. Bake until golden, about 25 minutes. (Adapted from a recipe by Kristy Carver - Edmond, OK) To make a MIX from this recipe, combine all but honey, buttermilk, and egg. Use within 1 month or refrigerate.)

CREPES

1/2 c. whole wheat flour	1 T. oil
1/2 c. water	1 T. dry milk powder
1/4 t. salt	3 egg whites or 2 eggs

Put all ingredients in blender and mix just until smooth. Pour scant 1/4 cup batter on lightly oiled hot skillet over medium heat. Lift and tilt skillet to spread batter. When batter dulls, turn over and cook just until lightly browned. Remove from pan. Place on a covered plate while others cook. Excellent filled with scrambled eggs made with onions, green pepper and a little picante sauce. Makes 12 crepes.

To freeze, put waxed paper or plastic wrap between each 4-5 cooked crepes. Wrap securely in plastic wrap, or place in plastic container. Use within 2 months.

SANDWICH FILLINGS AND SALADS

SEAFOOD SALAD FILLING

1/2 c. mayonnaise*	1/2 c. diced green onions
1/4 c. catsup	6 1/2 oz. can drained tuna in water
(opt)	
1 large diced tomato	2 c. cooked rice or cracked wheat
1/2 c. diced green pepper	1/2 c. diced celery

*Use regular or fat-free mayonnaise, or make your own. See page 123 for recipe.

Mix all ingredients well. Fill 6 pita pockets or use on toasted whole wheat bread. Serves 4.

TACO FILLING

1 c. cooked cracked wheat or rice   1/2 c. fat-free cottage cheese
1/4 t. cumin   1 T. chopped green chilies
1 T. parmesan cheese   1/2 c. chopped onion
salt to taste   2 T. water
                                      chopped lettuce leaves
                                          or alfalfa sprouts

Put water and onions in heavy skillet and steam for 1 minute over medium-high heat. Add remaining ingredients except lettuce and heat through. Use to fill flour tortillas, taco shells or pitas. Pack in plenty of lettuce or sprouts. Serves 4.

SUPER EASY SUN SALAD

2 c. 2-3 day sprouted sunflower seeds   1 T. lemon juice
1 t. olive oil

Mix all ingredients (add salt to taste) and serve plain or on a bed of lettuce or sprouts. Serves 4.

SPROUT SALAD

1 large bunch chopped lettuce   1 c. alfalfa sprouts
1 diced cucumber   1 grated carrot
1 c. mung bean sprouts   1 lg. diced tomato
2 T. lentil sprouts

Lightly toss all but alfalfa sprouts. Garnish with sprouts or freshly chopped chives. Top with your favorite dressing. Serves 6.

CREAMY RANCH DRESSING

2 c. mayonnaise
2 c. buttermilk
1/2 t. garlic powder
1 T. dried onion flakes

2 T. dried parsley
1/2 t. black pepper
1/2 to 1 t. salt

Put mayonnaise in a quart jar and stir while slowly adding buttermilk. When smooth, add remaining ingredients. Makes 1 qt. To make a MIX from this recipe, combine 12 x the amount of seasonings (12 T. dried onion flakes, etc.). To use, add 3 1/2 T. mix to 2 c. ea. mayonnaise and buttermilk.

EGGLESS MAYONNAISE

1 1/2 c. evaporated milk (12 oz. can)*
1 t. salt

1/3 c. lemon juice
1 3/4 c. vegetable oil

Place all ingredients in blender and blend until smooth. Makes 1 quart. You can also use soy milk (Nayonnaise) or almond milk (Almondaise).

BLENDER MAYONNAISE

2 eggs or 4 egg whites
1 t. salt
1 1/2-1 3/4 c. vegetable oil

2 T. lemon juice
2 T. white vinegar
1/8 t. white pepper (opt.)

Blend all except 3/4 c. oil until smooth. On high speed, slowly add the oil in a steady pencil-thin stream. Refrigerate and use within 2 weeks.

SUPER SPROUT MIX

2 T. lentils
2 T. adzuki beans
1 T. sunflower seeds

2 T. mung beans
4 T. wheat

Place seeds in quart jar in 2 c. water for 8 hours, or overnight. Drain well (use the water for plants or soup stock). Lay jar on its side in a dark, warm place. Rinse with lukewarm water 2 times a day for two days. Eat plain or with dressing, on sandwiches, sprinkled on salads or in soups just before serving. Excellent source of vitamin C, calcium, protein, and enzymes.

SPROUTED WHEAT

3/4 c. wheat

Quart jar method. Place seeds in quart jar in 2 c. warm water for 8 hours, or overnight. Drain well (use the water for plants or soup stock). Lay jar on its side in a dark, warm place. Rinse with lukewarm water 2 times a day for two days, draining well after each rinsing.

Plate and wick method. Place a wash cloth or piece of terry cloth on a plate. Sprinkle with unsoaked wheat so that kernels touch each other. Cover with another cloth. Rest plate on a shallow pan containing water, with one end of the cloth hanging down into the water. The cloth will act as a wick and draw up water to keep the wheat moist.

Eat plain or with dressing, on sandwiches, sprinkled on salads or in soups just before serving. Also excellent mixed with shredded coconut, and served over sliced bananas.

WHEAT GRASS

Under emergency conditions, if you have no other sprouting seeds, wheat must be sprouted to the grass stage to provide the body with a source of vitamin C to prevent scurvy.

On sprouting trays or baking sheet lined with 3 layers of paper towels, spread 6 c. wheat that has been sprouted 2 days. Kernels should barely touch. Cover wheat with 3 layers of paper towels. Place in a warm room, away from direct sunlight. Sprinkle with water several times a day to keep moist.

After 3 days, wheat sprouts will begin to push toweling up several inches. Remove toweling when wheat grass is about 4" tall, continuing to moisten sprouts several times daily. Cut and use grass when 4-7" tall. Blades of grass can be added to fruit or vegetable smoothies, sprinkled on salads, used as a lettuce replacement in sandwiches, or used to garnish soup.

MAIN DISH SOUPS

We can survive very well on simple foods—soups, meatless patties and other sandwich fillings, breads, and sprouts or vegetables. When I have had to use only the most basic stored foods in an emergency, or when our tough financial periods lasted longer than one year, our lunch was almost always a veggieburger or a filled pita pocket, and our evening meal was almost always soup. Soup is fast, filling, nutritious, and SO versatile! You can add a wide variety of ingredients to vary the flavor, color, texture, and thickness. Therefore, I have included my favorite hearty soups.

For faster cooking, grate or thinly slice vegetables, and coarsely crack beans and grains.

KRISTY'S RED BEANS AND RICE

2 c. pinto, pink or red beans   1 t. cumin
1/8 -1/4 t. crushed red pepper   4 T. beef or ham-flavored bouillon
1 clove garlic, minced   2 t. dried minced onions
***

2 c. rice

If using brown rice, soak overnight in 4 c. cold water. Soak rinsed beans overnight in 9 c. cold water. In the morning, add seasonings to beans and cook using one of the following methods (or rinse beans and pressure cook all but rice for 50 minutes in 9 c. warm water):

In a Pressure Cooker: Pressure cook 20 minutes at 15 lbs. pressure. Meanwhile, bring 2 c. white rice to a boil in 4 c. water, or the brown rice to a boil in soaking water. Cover pan, reduce heat to low, and cook 15-20 minutes. OR, thaw 4 c. frozen cooked brown rice. Add rice to cooked bean mixture or place a scoop of rice on top of each bowl of beans. Serves 4. For a little more flavor (and a lot more "heat"), add a few drops tabasco sauce to each bowl.

In a Saucepan: Cook over medium heat for 1 hour (covered) in soaking water. Add red pepper, garlic, and seasonings Cook 3 more hours.

HARVEST SPECIAL SOUP

We love to make this soup using our fresh garden produce.

4 c. boiling water
1 c. finely chopped onion
1/2 c. chopped bell pepper
2 c. red kidney beans, cooked
2 c. lima beans, cooked

2 c. chopped zucchini
1 c. chopped mushrooms
2 c. fresh or frozen corn
1 t. Worcestershire sauce
1 T. chicken or vegetable soup base
1 c. Jack cheese, grated (opt)

Combine water with fresh vegetables and cook over medium heat for 10 minutes, or until veggies are crunchy/tender. Add remaining ingredients, except cheese, and heat through. Serve topped with Jack cheese, if desired. Serves 6-8.

BEANS 'N BARLEY SOUP

1 qt. bottled tomatoes OR
   4 c. tomato juice
4 t. chicken or vegetable soup base
   (use only 1 t. base if tomato juice is used)

1/2 c. dry barley
1/2 c. dry cracked beans
1/2 t. crushed basil leaves

Bring all ingredients to a boil. Reduce heat to medium and cook, covered, for 30 minutes. If desired, add 2 c. fresh, frozen or cooked veggies just before end of cooking time. Serves 3-4.

CREAMY POTATO BISQUE

2 qt. boiling water
1 large onion, chopped
4 c. shredded potatoes
2 c. frozen peas

2 T. chicken or vegetable bouillon
1/2 t. pepper
1/3 c. white bean flour

In large saucepan over medium-high heat, cook first 3 ingredients until potatoes are tender, about 20 minutes. Add remaining ingredients, whisking in bean flour. Cook until thick, then reduce heat to low and cook, covered 5 minutes to blend flavors. Serve topped with fresh parsley. Serves 4-6.

MACARONI SOUP

2 qt. boiling water
1 c. shell macaroni
1 c. ea. chopped carrots, onion, celery, spinach, mushrooms, zucchini

2 T. chicken or vegetable bouillon
2 c. cooked garbanzo beans

Add all but cooked beans to boiling water and cook over medium heat for 10-15 minutes, or until macaroni is tender. Add cooked beans and simmer 5 minutes more. Serve topped with Parmesan cheese. Serves 4-6.

CREAMY TOMATO BASIL SOUP

4 c. boiling water
2 c. sprouted soy or white beans
2 c. tomato sauce

1-2 T. chicken or vegetable bouillon
1/4 lg. onion
1/8-1/4 t. basil

Cook beans and onion in water 15-20 minutes. Blend beans and onion in small amount of cooking water until very smooth. Pour into remaining water. Add tomato sauce and bouillon and heat through. Serves 3-4.

MEATLESS PATTIES AND LOAVES

CRACKED WHEAT OR RICE PATTIES

2 c. cooked cracked wheat or rice   1/2 c. chopped onion
2 T. dry milk powder   1 T. dried parsley
4 egg whites or 2 eggs   2 t. chicken or vegetable bouillon

Cracked wheat should be fairly dry and fluffy, like cooked rice. (See instructions above, in this section.) Mix all together. Drop by tablespoon onto skillet coated with cooking spray. Flatten to a round patty. Cover pan and cook until brown on both sides over medium heat. May be eaten hot or cold, plain or with cheese or gravy, or on a bun.

TACO SOYBEAN PATTIES

1 c. ground soaked soybeans   1 c. cooked cracked wheat
2 t. chicken or vegetable bouillon   1/2 c. onion, diced
4 t. taco seasoning   1/2 c. green pepper, diced
1 t. soy sauce   2 eggs
                                      1 c. bread or cracker crumbs

Sauté ground soybeans in 1 T. oil until lightly browned. Add to all other ingredients (reserving crumbs) and mix well.

Drop by tablespoon onto plate covered with crumbs. Press flat, turning to coat both sides. Place in hot skillet coated with cooking spray. Brown on both sides.

MINI WHEAT AND CHEESIES

2 eggs, or 4 egg whites, beaten   *2 T. grated onion*
1 1/4 c. fat-free cottage cheese   *1 c. water*
1/4 c. chopped green pepper   *1/4 c. dry milk powder*
1 t. chicken bouillon   *1 1/2 c. cooked rice or cracked whet*

Preheat oven to 350°F. Add dry milk powder to rice or wheat and stir well, then add beaten eggs and stir again. Add remaining ingredients. Mix, and pour into muffin tins coated with cooking spray; fill 3/4 full. Bake for 20-30 minutes. Note: Cheddar cheese may be substituted for cottage cheese. Top with white sauce, if desired.

BLENDER WHITE SAUCE

3 T. white bean flour   *1 c. boiling water*
  (or use whole wheat flour)   *3 T. butter or oil (opt.)*
2 T. dry milk powder   *1/2 t. salt*
  (or powd. non-dairy creamer)   *dash pepper*

Blend all ingredients and cook over low heat 3 minutes, stirring occasionally. Makes 1 1/4 c. sauce.

MINI WHEAT LOAVES MEXICANA

1 c. mild taco sauce   *3/4 c. oatmeal*
1 T. dried minced onion   *4 T. chopped ripe olives*
2 egg whites or 1 egg   *1 c. cooked rice or cracked wheat*
1/2 c. cottage cheese   *1/4 t. salt (opt.)*
1/2 t. each chili powder, cumin, oregano and basil

Mix all ingredients. Measure six 1/2 c. portions into large muffin tins coated with cooking spray. Bake at 375°F for 25 minutes. If loaves stick to the pans, let set 5 minutes before removing. Serves 6. If desired, top each Mini Loaf with 1 T. grated cheddar cheese during last 5 minutes of baking.

SNACKS

"POPPED" WHEAT

1 c. clean, dry whole wheat   *Salt*
Heavy, deep skillet   *Oil or butter*

Place wheat in skillet and place over medium-high heat. Shake or stir until wheat makes a "popping" sound and is slightly browned. (Some kernels may escape the pan, but not like popcorn.) Remove from heat, add oil or butter and salt. Or, add a little soy sauce and sprinkle with chili powder. If available, "pop" and add sunflower seeds, pumpkin seeds, instant brown rice, and toasted nuts.

TACO WHEAT NUTS

2 c. steamed wheat   *1 pkg. taco seasoning mix*

Combine steamed wheat (see recipe in this section) and seasoning mix. Process through a hand meat grinder (an excellent survival food processor!). Lift the little inch-long curls from the grinder as they come out, and place on baking sheets. Bake at 350° for about 30 minutes until crisp. If desired, add grated or powdered cheese before grinding. Experiment with other seasonings. The variety of tastes you can create is endless. For a dessert snack, try adding a little honey, vanilla, cinnamon, nutmeg, and powdered milk.

NUT AND RAISIN BALLS

In a blender, food processor or hand meat grinder, process 3/4 to 1 1/4 c. raisins, 1/2 c. 3-day wheat sprouts, and 1 c. raw or toasted nuts. Remove from blender and add 1/4 c. peanut butter. Knead well to mix. Press into an 8" square pan and cut into squares. Or, place in quart zip-loc bag and press flat. Eat within 2 days or wheat sprouts tend to harden.

For *Nutty Super Energy Bars*, combine 1 c. raisins, 1 c. nuts, 1/2 c. peanut butter, 1/2 c. honey, and 1/2 c. 3-day wheat sprouts. Process as above.

FRUIT SURPRISE

(Vary the flavor by varying the type of fruit and juice you add.)

1 c. water	*1/2 t. acidophilus powder (opt.)*
2 c. rice milk	*2 c. frozen fruit chunks*
1/2 c. pineapple or apple juice conc.	*2 t. flaxseed oil*
1/4 c. any kind of protein powder	*1/2 t. vitamin C*

Place all ingredients in blender and process until protein powder is no longer grainy. If desired, add 2 t. sunflower seeds and blend just enough to break them up. This is a good drink to hide a teaspoon or two of oat bran and wheat germ, too!

*Acidophilus powder is found at health stores and is a "friendly bacteria" that is necessary to fight off candida and other invaders.

GREAT WHEAT CHIPS

1 c. + 2 T. water	*1/2 c. whole wheat flour*
1 t. white bean flour	*1/2 t. any type seasoning blend*

Blend water and flours until smooth. Stir in seasoning. Spoon batter onto a baking sheet lightly coated with cooking spray. Sprinkle each circle of batter lightly with sesame seeds, poppy seeds, or Parmesan cheese.

Tilt pan to spread very thin, turning pan as you tilt to maintain circle shape. Bake at 350° for 8 minutes, or until edges curl and center is set. Turn over; bake another 2-5 minutes until golden and crisp.

DESSERTS

HONEY BUTTER

To turn hot bread into a dessert, there's nothing so wonderful as Honey Butter. In emergency conditions, you can omit the butter, whip the honey, and add flavored extracts such as coconut, pineapple, strawberry, raspberry, orange, etc. The amount you add depends on the flavor and the brand of flavoring.

1 c. light honey   *3/4 c. butter*

Warm honey and butter to room temperature. Using wire whip or electric beater, whip softened butter until light colored. Add honey, a little at a time, and whip until fluffy. Use within 1 week, or refrigerate. For Cinnamon honey butter, add 2 T. ground cinnamon. See **Natural Meals In Minutes,** p. 24, for Fruit Flavored Honey Butter recipes.

CRAZY STORAGE CAKE

This is a great storage cake because it doesn't require eggs and it can be easily adapted to the ingredients you have on hand. You can omit the ginger and molasses and add 3 T. carob or cocoa, or use grated orange peel and carob or chocolate chips. Add nuts instead of raisins..or bananas instead of applesauce...or just let your creativity run wild!

1 c. raisins or chopped dates	*1 t. salt*
2 c. boiling water	*2 t. vanilla*
3 c. whole wheat flour	*3 T. vinegar*
2 t. baking soda	*1/4 c. dark molasses*
2 t. powdered cinnamon	*3/4 c. honey, melted*
2 t. powdered ginger	*1/3 c. applesauce*
1 c. dry milk powder	*1/4 c. oil or applesauce*

In a separate bowl, combine raisins and water. Let sit 5 minutes while assembling other ingredients. Mix all dry ingredients. Make a nest in the center and add all moist ingredients. Stir lightly to mix. Pour into oiled 9" x 13" pan. Bake at 400° for 20 minutes, or until center is done. Serve with milk for breakfast or a snack, or frost and serve as dessert.

YUMMY CAROB CHIP COOKIES

1/2 c. olive oil
1/2 c. honey
1 t. vanilla extract
1 T. white vinegar
1/4 t. salt
1/4 c. grated carrots or applesauce*

1 t. grated orange peel*
1 c. whole wheat flour
2 c. rolled oats
1/2 t. baking soda
1/2-1 c. chopped nuts
1/2-1 c. carob or chocolate chips

Preheat oven to 350°F. In a medium bowl, beat all moist ingredients. Mix in dry ingredients. Drop dough by tablespoon onto baking sheets coated with cooking spray. Bake 10-12 minutes. Makes 2 dozen. *Substitutions:* Use either dried, reconstituted carrots or apples (blended to a sauce).

ESTHER'S APPLE BETTY

2 c. dried apple slices
2 1/2 c. water
1 T. cornstarch

1/3 c. honey
1 t. vanilla
1 t. cinnamon

Bring to a boil. Cover pan and reduce heat. Simmer 20 min. Place in 8" baking dish. Combine the following and sprinkle on top:

1/2 c. brown sugar or honey
1/2 c. oatmeal
1/3 c. butter, melted

1/2 t. cinnamon
1/2 c. whole wheat flour

Bake 15 min. at 350°F. Serve hot or cold; plain or with milk. Serves 6.

CREAMY 3-MINUTE PUDDING

2 c. hot water
1 T. butter (opt.)
1/3 c. honey (or sugar)
1/3 c. dry milk powder
(or powd. non-dairy creamer)

1 -2 eggs or 2 egg whites
1 t. vanilla
3 T. cornstarch
1/4 t. salt
1/8 t. lemon extract

Add butter (if used) and honey (or sugar) to 1 c. of the water and bring to a boil over medium heat. Mix remaining ingredients and water until free of lumps, using blender or wire whip. Stir into boiling water. Cook 1 minute. Serve hot or cold. Can be topped with fresh strawberries and Graham Cracker or Grape Nuts crumbs (See **Natural Meals** for recipes).

PIONEER RECIPES
OLD FASHIONED HONEY TAFFY

1 c. honey

Cook to hard crack stage at 285°F. Stir occasionally. Remove from heat and pour onto buttered platter. As outside edges cool, fold to the center and start stretching while still hot. Use a small amount of butter on hands to prevent sticking. Pull until light and porous and until small strings develop.

ALL-DAY SUCKERS

1 c. honey   *1 1/2 c. dry milk powder*
few drops peppermint oil

Cook honey to hard crack stage (when a small amount dropped into a glass of cold water can be gathered into a ball that makes a tinkling sound when hit against side of glass) at 285°F. Remove from heat and immediately stir in enough dry milk to make a stiff ball. Add peppermint oil to taste, and coloring, if desired. Roll into small balls, insert sucker sticks and allow to harden on a lightly oiled baking sheet.

WILD YEAST

2 c. flour   *2 t. honey*
2 c. warm water

Mix well and place in bottle or crock, uncovered. Allow mixture to ferment five days in a warm room. Stir several times a day with a non-metal spoon, thus aerating the batter and permitting the air to activate the mixture. It will smell yeasty, and small bubbles will come to the top.

Wild yeast is used in varying amounts in recipes for bread, rolls, hot cakes, etc. The fifth day, after using some, "feed" the starter (to replace the amount used in baking) using equal parts of flour and water or potato water. In another 24 hours the yeast will foam, and be ready for use again.

Store the unused portion of the yeast in refrigerator in a glass or crockery container with a tight-fitting lid. Shake it often. To activate it before using it again, add 2-3 T. flour and the same amount of water; stir well. (Without refrigeration, start can be kept "fresh" by using often.)

Some say the yeast spores around the crusty top of the container are beneficial and that one should not keep emptying and washing it.

SOURDOUGH BREAD

1 c. starter (wild yeast)   2 t. salt
2 c. warm water   2 T. dry milk
3 1/2 c. flour   1 T. honey

Mix well. Place ball of soft dough in a nest of flour. Knead in only enough flour to keep mixture from sticking. Develop the gluten for 10 minutes by kneading or pounding. Place the satin-smooth ball in a warm bowl and cover bowl with a hot, damp towel. Allow dough to rise for about 5 hours at room temperature (72°F), or until it doubles in bulk. (Five hours rising time is characteristic of sourdough bread made with wild yeast, which takes longer to rise than commercial yeast.)

Shape into 3 loaves and allow to rise again for about 3 hours (use small pans 3 1/2" x 7 1/2"). Bake at 325°F for about 1 hour in oiled pan or large juice cans.

COTTAGE CHEESE

2 c. dry milk   2 qt. water

Mix in blender, then allow to stand until form clabber is formed. (This may take 70 hours at a room temperature of 70°F, 50 hours at 85°F.) Add 2 qt. boiling water. Allow to stand 4-5 minutes, then gently pour off excess liquid and strain through cheese cloth or a colander. Add about a gallon of boiling water to the curd and allow to stand until it is set and has body. Drain and turn curd into a bowl. Add salt to taste, and buttermilk, if you have it.

CANNING WITHOUT ELECTRICITY

When my mother had a chance to get almost free vine-ripened tomatoes, she bought enough for 200 quarts (as a family, we tend to jump into things in a BIG way). Processing them in her 6-qt. canner would have taken forever. Instead, they bottled them all in one afternoon, outside, under the shade of a tree. They used two fifty-gallon metal barrels as "canners." They filled them with water, built a fire under each one, then:

1. Cleaned the jars and lids in hot water.

2. Scalded the tomatoes (one minute in hot water, then one minute in cold.

3. Skinned them and firmly packed them in quart bottles.

4. Added 1 t. salt per bottle, poured water in the bottle to within 1/2" of the top, and wiped off the seeds and pulp.

5. Put a new flat canning lid on and screwed the band firmly tight.

6. Carefully lowered the jars into the barrel of water so they didn't touch each other. (Small strips of wood separated the layers of bottles and were also put under the first layer of bottles to keep them from touching the bottom.)

7. Kept the hot water boiling around and over the top of all the bottles for about 35 minutes.

8. Removed the bottles and placed them on folded cloths. (The lids popped and went slightly concave, showing they were properly sealed.)

9. Carefully removed bands and lined jars up on cool, dark basement shelves.

This method works well for all fruits.

STEP 8

KEEPING CLEAN

Sanitation and Other Supplies

This is a small step, but oh, so important!!!!!!! While there are many products on the market to wash away (or cover up!) dirt and odors, keeping clean must also include reducing or eliminating harmful bacteria and viruses.

Keeping clean isn't just a "nice" thing to do. It may well be a life-saving measure. The "all-in-one" product I use AND store is GSE (NutriBiotic Liquid Concentrate Grapefruit Seed Extract). Because of its unique ability to destroy harmful bacteria, viruses and parasites, this powerful product is perfect for first aid as well as keeping clean. It has been found to be effective for acne, candida, colds and flu, cold sores, cuts and wounds, dandruff, diaper rash, diarrhea, earache, gingivitis, impetigo, poison oak, poison ivy, sinusitis, sore throat and ulcers. Quite a list!!!

GSE is also excellent as a vegetable/fruit or meat/poultry wash. Just a few drops even controls mold in humidifiers, vaporizers, water pik units and laundry. For information, call 1-888-232-6706.

Using regular soap, hands should be washed at least 20 seconds (the time it usually takes to sing "Happy Birthday" through twice!) to effectively kill harmful bacteria. Does anyone but a doctor wash that long?

An easier solution is to add several drops of GSE to liquid hand soap, or buy antibacterial hand soap. This is especially important during times of water shortage when we may not be taking full baths as frequently as usual.

OTHER ESSENTIALS FOR KEEPING CLEAN
Laundry soap for 100-150 loads of wash per person per year
1/2 gal. liquid hand soap or 15 bars of soap per person
2-3 gal. shampoo per person
hair spray - we use about 2 gal. per year for 3 adults
4 oz. NutriBiotic Liquid Concentrate per person (for disinfecting bodies, surfaces, purifying water, destroying internal bacteria, virus and parasites, and for washing wounds)
6 tubes toothpaste (6 oz. size) per person
4-6 toothbrushes per person
shaving supplies
  (My husband uses about 8 cans of shaving cream and 100 disposable
  raizors per year.)
3-4 containers deodorant per person
1-2 containers dental floss per person
shoe polish and brush or polishing cloths
one broom and dustpan
window cleaner
cleaning rags, towels, paper towels, washcloths

SANITARY SUPPLIES
I don't want to make my own sanitary napkins like my mother used to, so sanitary napkins and tampons are HIGH on my priority list!

What is a year's supply? Count how many you use in a month and multiply by 12. I most often buy more than a year's supply when I find them on sale.

Sanitary napkins also make excellent compresses to stop bleeding from a cut or other large wound

WASTE DISPOSAL
Proper sanitation techniques and disposal of waste may well save lives. Bacterial infections such as typhoid and dysentery can be just as devastating as the catastrophy that caused the emergency.

When water is cut off, toilets flush automatically when the bowl is filled with water, usually about 2-3 gallons. To avoid flushing after every use, add 10 drops GSE (Grapefruit Seed Extract) per use, close the lid, and flush only when solid waste is present.

We store the following "toilet"-ries for inside use:
toilet tissue - 50 rolls per person (phone books and catalogs are too
                    scratchy!)
6 boxes kleenex per person (a real luxury at my house!!)
4 oz. bottle NutriBiotic GSE (Grapefruit Seed Extract) - antibacterial, antiviral, antifungal - and ALL natural!

WHAT ABOUT WHEN YOU'RE CAMPING OR "ROUGHING IT?"
My sisters and I used to be disgusted at the thought of actually having to WIPE with the 6" squares of soft cloth my mother stored in suitcases down in the bomb shelter under our home. When we actually tried to store a full year's supply of toilet paper and kleenex, we finally began to understand the importance of having at least **some** alternatives on hand.

In other countries where my mother visited, it was a man's job to hand out single paper squares to men and women alike as they entered the public bathrooms. Thanks anyway, but if I'm going to be limited to one square, I'd rather have it be cloth than paper! I haven't quite come to terms with having to WASH those fabric squares, so I plan to have enough on hand to throw them away! I'm sad now to think of the suit-cases full of already cut soft cloth squares we got rid of when we turned mother's bomb shelter into a living area.

PORTABLE TOILET

A five gallon bucket has many uses. It can be a chair, a stool, a storage container for food or water, OR to store sanitary supplies. The following items could be stored in a heavy plastic bag inside the bucket:

2 boxes of garbage can liners (7-10 gallon size)
1 large piece heavy string or bungie cord
2 oz. bottle GSE (Grapefruit Seed Extract)
   for disinfecting and to kill all unwanted "bugs"
6-8 rolls toilet paper
2 lg. boxes baking soda
Soft cloth squares

To use the toilet, remove plastic bag with all contents. Place one liner inside, securing edges with the string or bungie cord. Mix 10 drops GSE liquid with 2 quarts water and pour into bucket to kill bacteria, viruses, and eliminate some of the odor. Our "Cadillac" model sports a cast-off toilet seat, secured to the top of the bucket by duct tape, but removed after each "sitting."

After each usage, sprinkle contents of bucket with baking soda and replace lid securely. When 1/3 to 1/2 full, bury it with at least 12 inches of earth, or place in an approved disposal location. NEVER deposit human waste on open ground. If you don't have plastic bags available, waste should be buried at least 24" deep.

MISCELLANEOUS TO KEEP RATS AND
OTHER CRITTERS FROM "TAKING OVER" THE HOUSE

   Rat poison
   Mouse traps
   Rat traps
   Boric Acid for cockroaches and pantry pests
   Fly swatters

SOAP MAKING

I don't like preparing meat to eat, and I really don't like handling the fat and "stuff" cut off of meat, so I prefer to buy and maintain a year's supply of soaps and non-soap cleaners and shampoos. For those of you who want to be REAL pioneers, like my baby sister Elizabeth who is not afraid to tackle anything, here are some simple instructions:

Equipment For Making Soap
   Container to make the soap in - 6 qt. size or larger
   It is best to use enamel, earthenware or granite containers,
      as the lye used in soap-making eats metal.
   Wooden stick or spoon to stir the soap
   Fine sieve or cheesecloth to strain the fat.
   Molds to pour the soap in, either enamel or glass, lined with waxed paper or a damp cloth. A box, milk cartons, or small glass molds of any kind can be used. If you don't want to use a mold, leave the soap in the pan until it sets, then turn it out and cut it in chunks.)

DIRECTIONS FOR MAKING LYE SOAP

Ingredients
   10 cups animal fat - melted, strained and clarified
   1 pound can of lye
   5 cups rain water or soft water
   1/2 c. powdered borax
   1/2 c. ammonia

Use only animal fat in this recipe. It can be rendered from meat fat. Don't overheat it. Strain in a fine sieve or a cheesecloth. To wash the salt out of fat which is salty, put fat in a pan, cover with cold water, and heat. Allow to cool, skim off the fat, and the salt and sediments will go to the bottom.

Now, only five easy steps remain:
   1. Warm fat to consistency of warm honey, so that it can be poured into lye mixture. (If fat is too hot it will curdle the soap.)

2. Put the 5 cups of water in the container.

3. Add lye to the cool water and stir vigorously until dissolved. (Don't stand over the mixture.) Add ammonia and borax, one at a time. Continue stirring until mixture is cool. (Lye heats the water.)

4. Pour fat into the lye mixture very slowly. Stir continuously for 15 minutes or until it is thick and creamy. (Don't over-stir.)

5. Pour the mixture into molds or flat pans, then allow to stand for a day or so until it is set. Cut into bars while it is medium soft, then wrap in waxed paper. It is ready for use in about a week. Some advise it should not be used for several months.

(p. 135-136, **Passport To Survival**, by Esther Dickey)

STEP 9

ENERGY

Heating, Cooking, Cooling, Lights

HEATING

There are many emergencies that could cause you to be without electricity. We may be able to survive fairly well without lights, but for most of us, the thought of being without heat in winter is unthinkable. Electric furnaces, gas furnaces with electric blowers, or even fireplaces with electric blowers would be useless or inefficient.

A generator to supply enough electricity to heat a home is expensive, and you would have to store fuel to operate it, an option that isn't available to apartment-dwellers or in most subdivisions. Installing a large outside propane tank to run small indoor heaters and cookstoves is also expensive. Most camp-type heaters are meant to be used *outside* because of the toxic fumes they produce. Burning charcoal inside could be fatal! Most fireplaces are built for show. At best, they may heat only the room in which they are located. At any temperature below freezing, it doesn't take long to cool a house down to a very uncomfortable temperature.

What's the solution? The object in preparing for keeping warm in periods without power, especially in the dead of winter is not to prepare to heat a whole house comfortably, but to provide enough heat to keep you alive. The easiest solution is to divide off one room with mylar "space blankets" and then stock up on a stove that burns clean-burning fuel.

Wood-burning stoves are ideal because they produce great amounts of heat. Stoves that are fire-brick lined will also burn coal. Caution: Check with the installer or manufacturer to make sure your stove can withstand the extra heat coal produces. Before installing a wood-burning stove in your home, check to see if there are laws prohibiting its use. Check building codes to see how far stove pipes have to be from the wall and what type of chimney is acceptable.

Most stoves have a cooking surface large enough for at least 2 pans to quickly boil water or cook food. Metal "ovens" for baking breads can be purchased to set on top of a stove. I thoroughly enjoy cooking on a wood stove, whether I'm slowly simmering a pan of soup or beans on top; drying fruits and vegetables underneath or near the ceiling; or culturing milk on the side to make yogurt or cheese.

Wood should be stacked and covered to keep it dry. If you use coal regularly, it can be piled on the ground and covered to keep dry. Coal to be stored should be placed in a plastic-lined pit, or in sheds, boxes or barrels and should be covered to keep out circulating air, light and moisture. How much do you need? It depends on the severity of your winters and how well your home is insulated. When we lived in the mountains of Colorado, we used a free-standing wood/coal stove to heat our home, burning at least a ton of coal each year, in addition to 2 cords of wood. In Oklahoma, using a standard inefficient fireplace with an electric blower, we burn about 5 cords of wood to heat our house each year. Coal is not available. We are in the process of getting another alternate heating source to use if we no longer have electricity for the blowers.

Kerosene heaters are fairly inexpensive and do a good job of producing heat. On some models, you can warm a pan of water or food on top of the heater. Purchase only K-1 rated kerosene, as other lower grades produce a stronger odor. Kerosene is not explosive, so is safer to store than gasoline or Coleman fuel. A 55-gallon plastic drum or the equivalent in 5-gallon plastic containers should last an entire winter if used sparingly. Burning kerosene (and propane) consumes oxygen and produces carbon monoxide, so make sure to leave one or two windows open about an inch to circulate some fresh air.

Propane heaters burn clean enough for indoor use. Again, open a window just a crack when burning propane. Propane stores indefinitely. Check with the fire marshall in your area to find out if propane can be stored where you live. Using a small 10,000 BTU propane heater connected to a 5-gallon propane bottle would provide heat for about 3-4 days when used sparingly. **Propane camp stoves** are easy to use and the most like what we are used to using every day. When used indoors, they provide heat for cooking while also warming a room.

Burning materials need not be limited to wood, coal, kerosene or propane. Check cabinet shops, pallet manufacturing companies and construction sites for burnable scraps. Other burnable materials include nut shells, peach and apricot pits, corn cobs, dry bones, black walnuts, acorns and pecans, dried stalks from corn and Jerusalem artichokes, or newspaper "logs." To make **newspaper "logs,"** use six sections (five double sheets in each section) for each log. With double sheets folded to page size, fold in halves once, then again, each section separately. Stack the sections up, alternating cut sides with folded ones, and with the bottom section extending out about 5". Roll very tight; secure in the center of the roll with a piece of florist's wire. Four logs last about one hour.

Don't forget to store several boxes of "strike anywhere" matches! Another valuable addition is sheets or rolls of plastic, or plastic tarps that can be used to divide off rooms into smaller sections to maintain heat.

COLD-WEATHER CLOTHING

To survive cold weather in relative comfort, make sure you have heavy wool stockings, gloves or mittens, hats and scarves, in addition to a coat heavy enough to keep the air from whistling through when you are outside. Dress in layers so you can quickly adapt your attire to the different temperatures usually encountered when going from outside to inside, round about and back again.

COOKING

If your emergency occurs during the winter, you will need fuel for at least some of your cooking. It is best to plan on cooking outside, where you have more choices in the type of fuel used. In the summer, you can construct a solar oven (See Chapter 4 for detailed instructions.). In addition to the fuels listed above, consider the following:

Sterno is a jelled petroleum product and usually is included in 72-hour kits because it is light weight and easy to start with a match or a spark from flint and steel. It is not explosive and is safe to use indoors. A sterno stove can be purchased for under $10. Because the fuel evaporates easily, it is not good for long-term storage.

White gas (Coleman fuel) is readily available. It needs to be used and stored outside, but produces a hot flame and cooks food quickly.

Check out the inherent hazards of whatever heating or cooking options you choose. Have a fire extinguisher handy, and make sure everyone knows how to use it. Don't ever go to sleep with any of these heating or cooking devices burning (except a standard fireplace or properly installed wood/coal stove). There are too many chances for fire or asphyxiation.

Besides **matches,** other possible fire starters include **small limbs and twigs, paper goods** and **most dry household garbage, dryer lint,** a **candle,** and **00 size steel wool** placed between **2 flashlight batteries** to create a spark.

ALTERNATIVE COOKING METHODS AND EQUIPMENT

People have cooked food without either electricity or gas, and even without pots and pans. Get a group of people together and explore a variety of ways to cook without electricity. The following alternative outdoor cooking methods can be used for camping, cookouts, or for a "roughing it" practice run...for the experience and for *hours* of entertainment!

CLAY - Cover a potato with stiff, moist clay about 1" thick. Bake in hot ashes. The clay will come away easily when potato is cooked through.

LEAVES - Bake biscuits between several layers of sweet green leaves placed on hot ground and covered with ashes and hot coals.

PIT - Lee Bean, my Maori brother-in-law, provided this information on pit cooking, called a haungi or luau by the people of Polynesia. Dig a pit big enough to hold a whole beef or small enough for a bird. Line with bricks, rocks or metal (anything that retains heat). Build a bonfire in it of pine and fast-burning woods. Let it burn for about 1 1/2 to-3 hours. Windy days help raise the heat quickly. Rake coals out of pit.

Cover with a thin layer of something similar to tea leaves, banana leaves, corn husks, or other clean, damp leaves to keep the food clean. Add meat, potatoes, carrots, corn, onions, etc. Cover with more leaves. Damp sheets or burlap also work well. Cover with dirt. Food will cook through in about 3 hours, but can be left for 12 hours or more. It won't burn, but it may dry out a little. Pit cooking works best in warm weather and at lower elevations.

REFLECTOR OVEN - Anything shiny in front of a fire will reflect heat rays and thus will hasten cooking. A reflector oven can be improvised using a five-gallon can or from a box covered in aluminum foil.

ROCKS - Mankind has found uses for rocks in cooking since time began. The aborigines of Australia cooked kangaroos by filling their bodies with hot rocks. My brother, Neldon, wraps hot rocks from the fire in foil, puts them in the cavity of a chicken with seasoning salt, bouillon, or other seasoning. He then wraps it in foil, and newspaper or dry leaves to insulate. The chicken is placed in a plastic bag, where it cooks in 3-4 hours.

To cook steaks, set clean, smooth river rocks in a hot fire for 1 hour. Brush off, coat with cooking oil, and lay meat on top. Cook as you would in a skillet.

STEAM COOKING - Line a small pit with hot rocks from a fire. Place food between layers of damp grass or leaves, and put on top of rocks. Cover the top layer of grass with dirt. Make a hole down through the layers with a stick, pouring a small amount of water through this hole onto the hot stones. Repeat several times.

STICKS AND WOOD

• Bread On A Stick - When I was a little girl, making fresh bread wrapped on a stick was my favorite part of camping. If you have an open fire, you can make a pot of soup and wrap bread on a stick for a complete meal. Select a "green" branch, and remove the outer bark. (If you use a dried branch, you're likely to burn up the stick AND the bread!)

Shape yeast bread dough or baking powder biscuit dough into a long "snake" and wrap around branch, leaving 1" of space between twists. Lay stick over the fire, propped on "Y" shaped sticks pounded into the ground on both sides of the fire. Turn occasionally for even baking. When the dough is browned on the outside, the inside is usually done. Peel off and enjoy!! (Bread will cook faster if the branch is warmed over the fire first before being wrapped with dough.)

• String a line of little fish or frogs on a stick and cook over hot coals.
• Run a peeled stick through a chicken and use as a spit.
• Make a shish kebab by taking a two-foot straight stick about the diameter of a pencil, threading it alternately through small slices of meat and vegetables, and broiling the food over hot coals.
• Put a tiny stick through an egg (boring a hole with a sharp knife tip), and turn it over hot coals for about 10 minutes.
• Peg food on preheated hardwood sticks. Lean the sticks in front of a bank of glowing coals to cook the food.

FOIL

Keep a supply of aluminum foil on hand. Foil dinners are one of our favorites because you wrap up almost anything in foil, throw it on the coals in the fireplace or wood stove, and in 10-15 minutes, dinner is ready, with only one turning! (Buy a large, industrial size box of foil!)

• Assemble meat (if used), onion slices, potato and carrot slices in 3-4 layers of 12" square pieces of aluminum foil. Seal the package securely and bake in hot ashes for about 15 minutes, turning once.

• Using the above method, cook eggs, apples, or biscuits. If you don't have foil, you can cook in half of an orange peel, using the other half as a "lid!"

BUDDY BURNER - In a shallow tuna can, place a strip of corrugated cardboard cut to the height of the can. Pour melted paraffin to partially fill can. Allow to harden. Placing a birthday candle in the center will help to light the stove. You can control the heat by placing a lid on the can, secured with a wire handle.

VAGABOND STOVE - Use a number 10 (gallon) can. Punch holes around the top and bottom of the opened can with a can opener punch to provide a draft for your fire. Place the Buddy Burner (above), a can of Sterno "canned heat," or a 3-4 burning briquettes in the bottom (Start briquettes with 2/3 of a can of tightly wadded newspaper and very small kindling. They are ready to use when the outside turns to a grey ash.). Cook on top. If fire is too low, add rocks or pieces of bricks to the bottom to elevate.

FIRELESS COOKER, the original "crock pot!" - Insulating a lidded container of boiling-hot food helps maintain that temperature for 4-5 hours. Heavy cooking pans or crockery work best, but even a gallon can with a plastic lid will do. These fantastically simple fuel-saving devices are easy to put together.

Start with a heavy box. An apple or orange box, liquor box, wooden crate or a bushel basket will all work well. Insulate the inside of the container with an outer layer of folded newspaper, then tightly crumbled newspaper, forming a cavity in the middle by wrapping a heavy towel around your cooking container, placing it in the center of the box, then stuffing more paper tightly around it. Cover with an additional 4" layer of folded papers. Wrap the entire cooker with a blanket (wool or mylar works best).

Now you're ready to cook! Leaving the towel in place to help restrict air circulation, remove the pan. Grains, cracked beans, and small pieces of meat should be boiled for 5 minutes, then placed in the Fireless Cooker for 4-5 hours, or overnight. Whole beans should be boiled for 15 minutes before being placed in the Cooker. After 12 hours, a properly insulated pan of food cooked in this way is still steaming hot.

CHARCOAL OVEN - Use a heavy cardboard box (like a liquor box) that has been cut on three sides to create a hinged lid on top. Cover the whole thing with aluminum foil, inside and out. Tip the box so that the hinge is on the top and the door opens up from the bottom. Put some brick pieces on the bottom of the box and put a cookie sheet on top of that to use as a rack for holding whatever you're going to bake.

Heat charcoal briquettes according to instructions for Vagabond Stove above. Each briquette equals 40°F, so if you want to bake rolls at 400°F, you will need 10 briquettes. When the briquettes are ready, put them in your oven under the cookie sheet. Place whatever you are baking on the rack. You can place dough or bread pans, etc. directly on the rack. Prop the door open just a little so the briquettes can draw the necessary air for burning. It may be necessary to rotate items once or twice to make sure they cook evenly.

DUTCH OVEN - Check out prep@ldscn.com to subscribe to a dutch oven cooking newsgroup. There are a variety of cookbooks available on the internet and from your local library. The best ovens are made of cast iron, have a flat lid that allows you to fill it with briquettes, and legs on the bottom to allow you to stack smaller ovens on top of larger ovens to conserve fuel. More heat should be placed on top. For a 350° oven, add briquettes to equal the diameter of the oven $^+$5 for the top, and $^-$3 for the bottom. If you have a 12" oven, you would use 17 briquettes for the top, and 9 for the bottom. Bake for 45-50 minutes. You can raise the temperature by adding or subtracting 2 briquettes for every 25°. More is not better, however. To avoid burning your food, cook longer, not hotter!

To prevent hot spots in breads, cakes, etc., lift and rotate the oven 1/4 turn every 10-15 minutes, and then rotate lid 1/4 turn in the opposite direction. About 2/3 of the way through cooking time, remove the oven from the bottom heat. Food is usually cooked 5 minutes after you can start to smell it.

SOLAR OVEN - Solar ovens can be used 6-12 months out of the year, depending on where you live. My first experience with solar cooking was with a kit I purchased from Solar Cookers International, 1919 21st Street, Sacramento, CA 95814. You can e-mail them at sci@igc.apc.org. They sell the complete kit or a 1/8 scale mini-model and instructions to put together your own. You can also find information on many different types of solar cookers on the internet. One site has several good designs, but my favorite is the "Minimum" Solar Box Cooker at www.accessone.com/~sbcn/minimum.htm.

All it takes is *two large, shallow cardboard boxes* (one about 1" to 2" smaller than the other to allow for airspace between them, and just deep enough to hold the largest pot you will use), *one sheet of cardboard* to make lid and drip pan, *one small roll of aluminum foil, one can of flat-black spray paint* (non-toxic when dry), or *tempera paint*, and *one sheet of glass* or *one Reynolds Oven Cooking Bag®*. Almost any size oven will cook, but larger, shallow ovens get hotter and can cook more food.

Close the flaps on the larger box. Set smaller box on top. Draw around the outside of smaller box, then cut a hole in flaps of larger box (Fig. 1). If smaller box is too deep, slit at corners. Then draw a firm line along where you want the box to fold, bending sides back to form extended flaps (Fig. 2). Glue foil to inside of both boxes and remaining top flaps of outer box.

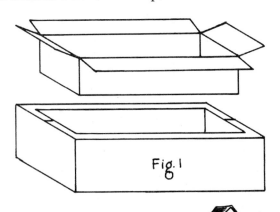

Fig. 1

For support, place a long *strip of cardboard (1-2" wide)*, folded into "W" shape, on floor of outer box. Fill in spaces with

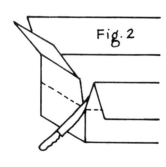

Fig. 2

tightly wadded newspapers. When inner box is set inside hole, flaps should barely touch top of outer box (Fig. 3). Glue flaps onto top of outer box and trim excess flap length even with perimeter of outer box.

Lay the sheet of cardboard on top of base, orienting the corrugations so they go from side to side as you face the oven. Trace the outline of the base, adding about 1/4" all around, and then score on those lines. Fold down edges about 3" over the sides of the larger box, forming a lid (Fig. 4). Fold corner flaps around and glue to sides of lid flaps.

To make reflector flap, draw a rectangle slightly smaller than the inside box. Cut on left, right and front sides, then open lid and bend back (Fig.5).

Fig. 3

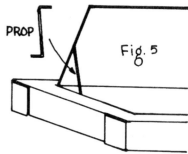

Fig. 4

To make a prop, cut a *12" piece of wire hanger* and bend 1" of one end forward, the other backward. This can then be inserted into the corrugations of the lid and door to prop door open to reflect sunlight.

Line underneath side of door with foil. Lay a piece of *glass* (tape the edges to avoid cuts) over outside of lid opening, or tape or glue an *oven bag* over inside of the opening. If you use the whole bag, be sure to tape or glue open end of bag shut so air is not trapped inside.

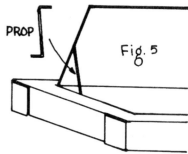

PROP

Fig. 5

To make drip pan, cut a *piece of heavy cardboard,* the same size as bottom of interior of oven (or use metal baking sheet), and apply foil to one side. Paint foiled side black and allow to dry. Put in oven (black side up) and place pots on it when cooking.

Sunlight penetrates the glass cover of the box and is absorbed by the black of the drip pan. The reflective surface of the door concentrates more heat, producing a cooking temperature of about 325°F. Cook in dark pots. Cast iron works best. Bright sun works best, but hazy days are okay. Start cooking early in the day. More food takes more time. Use hot pads, because the oven gets HOT! You may have to move the oven to follow the sun.

Solar Bean and Barley Soup - Combine 1 c. dry washed pinto beans, 1/3 c. dry barley, 3 c. water, 1/2 t. each cumin, oregano, chili powder and salt, and 1 large chopped onion. Bake for 4-5 hours.

Corn Casserole - In a small dark roaster coated with olive oil, combine 1 1/2 c. fresh or frozen (thawed) corn, 1/2 c. chopped green pepper, 1 small chopped onion, 1/2 c. dry cracked wheat, and 3 T. dry milk powder OR white bean flour. Combine the following and pour over the top: 2 eggs, beaten, 1 3/4 c. water, and 2 t. chicken bouillon. Cover and bake for 2 hours.

To pasteurize water, heat until bubbles are rising steadily from the bottom, about 150°F. Keep at that temperature for at least 30 minutes. In general, about 1 gallon can be pasteurized in about 3 hours on a day with strong sunlight, the sun high in the sky. This process kills germs and disease-carrying organisms including bacteria, rotaviruses, enteroviruses, and cysts commonly transmitted in contaminated water. This water is not sterile, and should not be used for medical procedures. It does not remove chemical contamination such as pesticides and industrial wastes.

COOLING
In 1974 when we lived in Texas, our whopping $50 a month air conditioning bill was the topic of much conversation among family members living in Oregon where most people didn't have or need air conditioning. In Oklahoma, there were some months during 1998 when paid close to $300 a month!. Air conditioning is a great blessing, but what would we do without it? Several people in Oklahoma died without it in this

year's series of scorching 100°+ temperatures. In my mother's day, several big cool, leafy shade trees shaded nearly every house in town. Houses were built to utilize cooling breezes. Porches on the north or east provided cool air for sleeping or lounging. (Mom, at 83, still sleeps outside year-round, thanks to a well-positioned sleeping porch with glass on one side to shield her from the worst of the wind, sleet, snow and rain, yet still allows her to see the beauty around her.) Today, houses are rarely insulated well enough or designed to fit into the environment.

In **Skills For Survival,** pp. 39, 40, you will find detailed instructions on how to build a KAP (Kearny Air Pump), resembling a venetian blind and installed in an open doorway. The frame is made of wood, hinged on the top, with thin, flexible plastic louvers made from heavy clear plastic table covering material available from fabric stores. A pull-cord is attached to the center, near the top.

Like the people in charge of keeping the kings of ancient times cool with fans made of palm fronds or feathers, someone needs to be in charge of pulling on the cord to make the Air Pump work. (Speaking of fans, it's a good idea to have several on hand, or know how to make them from lightweight materials.) In cold weather, you could move warm air heated by a wood stove or fireplace to colder parts of the house.

HOT WEATHER CLOTHING

You can take off only so much clothing to try to keep cool. What then? My sister, Elizabeth, on a month-long survival trip, said people wore buckskin (soft leather) shirts to provide protection against both cold and heat. Wetting the shirts with water provided them with a small period of cool comfort, even on the hottest days. Wool and cotton clothing work in much the same way.

Most of the clothing my mother wears as she scurries up stairs and down, inside and out, pulling, pushing, lifting and shoving all day long, is made of loose woven cotton to allow for the maximum amount of air movement, and most of it white to reflect light, and to allow her to bleach out the stains she collects. When we went shopping for fabric or clothing, my sisters and I used to laugh as she held up a single thickness of fabric and blew through it to determine if it was a loose enough weave. It didn't take very long, living in hot climates, to appreciate what she taught us about choosing "breathable" clothing so we can work and play in comfort.

I recently spent two weeks in a hot climate where there wasn't any air conditioning and the temperature was a humid 85°. Though I thought I'd suffocate at first, I did get somewhat used to it. When I returned home, the normal 75° setting on our home thermostat nearly froze me out! I cranked it up to 80° and was very comfortable. I found out later that it does take about 2 to 2 1/2 weeks for the body to acclimate to a change in temperature, hot or cold, but the body takes care of this on its own..no help needed from us. What a magnificent machine!

My sister, Leila, cools herself off by draping a wet cloth around her neck. It doesn't take much air movement to notice a comfortable drop in temperature.

LIGHTING

What will you do when the lights go out? It seems that no matter where we live, we always spend a few days each year without electricity. The flashlight we have plugged into the wall, designed to turn on when the power goes off, works very well...but not for very long. We always keep several flashlights and extra bulbs and batteries on hand, but even those don't last forever. What if you are without power for weeks...or months? Most of these alternatives use a real fire and flame, so be sure to teach proper safety procedures and have lots of "practice runs" to try out and perfect your creations and to become skilled at using them.

CANDLES
Everyone can afford candles. As mentioned earlier, seasonal candles go on sale several times each year. Buy white or light-colored candles and sturdy broad-based holders. The light they produce can be increased by placing them in front of a mirror or a shiny aluminum foil reflector.

While candles don't produce very **much** light, they are still better than nothing. Regular candles burn for about 4-5 hours. Store 365 candles, one for each day. You would need only about 40 "fatty" candles (50+ hours burning time).

TIN CAN LANTERN

As children, we loved making lanterns and lamps for our camping trips. A big part of the fun and excitement was getting to use "crafty" skills to make something useful...that actually worked! My favorite was the Tin

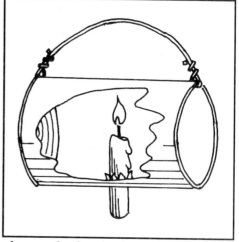

Can Lantern because the flame didn't go out easily. We even had contests, swinging the lanterns around in a circle, to see if any of us *could* put out the flame.

Lay a large *tomato juice or gallon coffee can* on its side. Cut an "X" in the middle of the side, bending back the cut edges, then pushing a 6" candle part way through the opening. When lit, the flame should not touch the top of the can. A handle was made by attaching a *cord or wire* to a small hole punched in both ends of the can. As the candle burns, push it further inside.

BOTTLE OIL LAMP

These are sold commercially, but can be easily made using a *clear glass pint or quart jar*, and some inexpensive supplies. It is safe to use indoors and puts off about as much light as a regular candle.

Form an "X" of *two nails*, about 1/2" smaller than the diameter of the jar. Tie them together with a *6" piece of 1/8" cotton string or candle wicking*. Bend top nail up slightly in the center so both ends touch the bottom of the jar. Bend a *12" piece of fine wire* in half and wrap it once around the center of the nails. Wind one end around the wicking going clockwise, the other counterclockwise, to help the wick stand up straight. Place in bottom of jar. Fill jar to within 1/2" from the top of the wick with cooking oil, olive oil preferred because it burns cleanest.

WARNING
Do NOT use kerosene, diesel fuel, or gasoline. Use only kitchen oils.

FOR A REFLECTOR, ATTACH ALUMINUM FOIL TWO THIRDS OF THE WAY AROUND JAR (LEAVING ONE THIRD UNCOVERED) AND UNDER ITS BOTTOM. AND TO THE WIRES. (FOIL IS NOT ILLUSTRATED.)

LOOP TO HANG LAMP (LARGE ENOUGH FOR FINGER)

TO LIGHT LAMP, FIRST MAKE MATCH LONGER BY TAPING OR TYING IT TO A STICK. TO EXTINGUISH, DRIP OIL ON WICK.

LIGHT WIRE

CLEAN GLASS JAR FREE OF LABELS

FILL JAR NO MORE THAN HALF-FULL WITH COOKING OIL OR FAT

FLAME FROM END OF WICK IS JUST ABOVE OIL SURFACE

A FINE WIRE TIED IN ITS CENTER AROUND THE NAILS, WITH THE ENDS OF THE WIRE WOUND IN OPPOSITE DIRECTIONS AROUND THE COTTON-STRING-WICK. USE COTTON THAT IS SLIGHTLY LESS THAN 1/8-in. IN DIAMETER. USE WINDOW SCREEN WIRE OR OTHER EQUALLY FINE WIRE.

BENT NAIL, TIED OVER TOP OF ANOTHER BENT NAIL, SO THE BASE WILL NOT ROCK.

USE NAILS ABOUT 1/2-in. SHORTER THAN THE DIAMETER OF JAR

KEEP EXTRA WIRE AND WICK-STRING IN SHELTER

WIRE-STIFFENED-WICK LAMP

To hang your lamp, place another *12" piece of wire* around the neck of the jar and twist loosely. *Bend two 18" pieces of fine wire* in half, stick your finger through the bend, and twist, forming a loop large enough for your finger to carry, or to hang on a hook or a nail. Slip one piece of this wire through the loose piece of wire around the neck, and twist to secure. Repeat with 3 remaining pieces.

To light, use a long fireplace match, or tape a match to a stick. To extinguish, drip oil on burning wick.

For best light, secure a *piece of aluminum foil,* shiny side touching the jar, 2/3 of the way around the jar, under the bottom, and part way up the wires.

KEROSENE LAMPS
These provide the most light, but also put off the most fumes and odor, especially if wicks are not properly trimmed and maintained. We have found numerous lamps at garage sales and thrift stores, but a new lamp can usually be purchased for under $10.

They will usually burn for about 45 hours on a quart of fuel. Ultra-Pure Candle and Lamp Oil burns cleaner and is less likely to cause strong odors and smoke. Wicks should be trimmed after each 12 hours of operation in the shape of an arch, a V, an A, or straight across. Be sure to stock up on extra wicks.

PROPANE AND WHITE GAS LANTERNS

Camp lanterns that burn white gas (Coleman fuel) and propane are by far the brightest, and put off the most heat (helpful in the cold!). They can be used indoors as long as adequate ventilation is provided. Tape extra packages of mantels (the white net bags that you "light") to the bottom of each lantern.

Caution: Fill and light lanterns outside in case of fuel spills or flash fires. Bring inside only after a few seconds of burning time. Never go to sleep with any of the above devices burning.

LIGHT STICKS

Cyalume sticks are usually sold in grocery stores at Halloween time. To activate, bend the plastic stick until glass tube inside breaks, then shake for a few seconds to produce light for up to 8 hours. The light is faint at best, and dims over time. The only real value in these sticks is to provide a "glow in the dark" light to mark a path, or to signal to another person. Don't plan on reading by them! They are good in 72-hour kits.

POP CAN CANDLE-LAMP

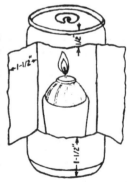

Using an empty standard *aluminum pop can,* you can make a sturdy candle holder. Using a small very sharp knife, cut a "window" in the can and bend back flaps. Place enough *sand or dirt* in can bottom to stabilize. Place *short candle* inside.

Warning: Candles are the safest non-electric lights to use indoors, but can produce enough carbon monoxide in a small shelter area to cause headaches.

Kearny, **Nuclear War Survival Skills**, U. S. Department of Energy, p. 149.

STEP 10

EMERGENCY DOCTORIN'

Learning to "listen" to the body's signals, rather than suppressing them, is essential to good health. Eating right, exercising, and positive thinking are just part of the total health picture. We are each born with inherent weaknesses, and we will all have accidents and injuries that require first aid. We will all experience some common acute ailments like colds, flu, and a sore throat now and then. Better health would help in coping better with the stress and strain of any emergency. The key is to be familiar with the treatment for common problems and start using it as soon as symptoms first develop, rather than waiting until the body is so worn down that it can't easily heal itself.

The key is to do something that will HELP the body cleanse itself of the accumulated toxins that have allowed illness to take over, rather than using invasive drugs that merely force the symptoms to move somewhere else.

Most illnesses can be treated without antibiotics, if treatment is started early to give the body's immune system a chance to take over. The regular over-use of antibiotics has created "super strains" of drug-resistant bacteria that are almost impossible to eradicate. The American Medical Association has declared this to be a serious health problem. The organization has initiated programs to educate doctors on alternatives to the use of antibiotics for every ailment. According to Dr. David G. Williams, author of <u>Alternatives</u> newsletter, life-threatening bacteria are showing up at a rate never before seen in human history. A new strain of *Salmonella typhrimurium* which is resistant to 98.8 percent of all antibiotics infected 4,000 people last year in Great Britain. This strain has now been directly linked to the use of antimicrobial drugs in the livestock industry.

Incidences of Hepatitis A and B are increasing dramatically. In 1997, there were more deaths from drug-resistant tuberculosis (TB) than ever before. The World Health Organization has declared TB to be a global emergency because it is one disease that has crossed virtually all borders.

Food poisoning is causing widespread panic in Japan, where 9,400 cases, apparently linked to a mutant strain of *E. coli,* were reported, with 11 deaths. The sudden emergence of these mutated strains are often traced to the overuse and misuse of antibiotics. Is it any surprise that the people who are suffering the most are those who live in wealthier countries like the United States?

Enterococci is a bacterium that causes serious, life-threatening staph and strep infections that has never responded to penicillin, but could be easily eliminated with the drug vancomycin...until 1988. Nearly ALL vancomycin-resistant enterococci (VRE) are acquired in hospitals, most in the intensive care units. People who previously used vancomycin were much more likely to acquire VRE.

"Dr. Sachs estimates that the average person will have consumed over 1000 doses of antibiotics by the time he or she reaches 50. Even more alarming, the average child has received over 200 doses of antibiotic treatment by age 3, each of which offers the possibility of a toxic reaction to the drugs." (The GSE Report, Vol 1., Issue 1)

The wholesale slaughter of ALL bacteria that occurs when taking an antibiotic eliminates the "friendly bacteria" that are supposed to protect the body, and upsets the delicate balance in the intestinal tract. Since it is almost impossible to destroy 100% of the offending bacteria, leaving behind even a few drug-resistant survivors can have disastrous effects. Without the natural balance of helpful bacteria, the resistant mutants double in population every few minutes and spread through your system in record time* (Dr. Williams). This method of treating *symptoms* rather than the *cause* of disease suppresses the immune system and "weakens some of the organs most needed to fend off potentially harmful microbes."* Dr. Allen Sachs, The Authoritative Guide to Grapefruit Seed Extract.

Home health care places the responsibility for better health on the individual...not on someone else. Wholesome foods, especially those rich in vitamins, minerals and essential enzymes (found only in raw foods), can only go so far in preventing or healing disease. But that doesn't mean we must accept illness and aging as a necessary part of life. Our bodies are *supposed* to be self-sustaining. Using just a few simple remedies, most people can go their whole lives without having to rely on prescription drugs. Yes, it takes time, effort and a lot of trial and error to learn how to use simple herbs and other remedies from the plant kingdom, but once you develop a program that's right for you, you'll never again need to give someone else control of your health.

ALTERNATIVES TO CONSIDER
Better Nutrition. "The evidence is irrefutable! Research from around the world and from the American Cancer Society and the National Cancer Institute in the U.S. agree...five servings a day of nature's disease fighters (raw fruits and vegetables) [and all raw sprouts] would markedly

reduce cancer...stroke...and heart disease, the leading killers of our times." (Dr. Sydney Crackower, M.S., M.D., Two M.D.'s And A Pharmacist Ask, "Are You Getting It Five Times A Day?") The awesome power of fresh, live foods is only now beginning to be recognized by the medical profession.

Eating whole foods, in their most natural state (preferably raw or lightly steamed) helps build better health by balancing the immune system to be better able to handle disease and all kinds of stress. Start now to improve the quality of your food to give your body the best chance possible to be healthy and whole.

Nutritional Supplements. Recent studies have exposed the damage done to the body by taking isolated vitamins and minerals as supplements, rather than obtaining them in their natural state - the foods in which they reside. My recommendation is to use and store Juice Plus+, a whole-food supplement made from the dried juice and fiber of whole fruits and vegetables. This product is packed with enzymes, antioxidants and naturally-occurring vitamins and minerals to ensure good nutrition and get your body's immune system back on track so it can fight against disease and aging. For information, call 1-888-232-6706.

Antimicrobial Grapefruit Seed Extract (GSE). 100% effective at killing dozens of bacteria, fungi, viruses, yeast and other harmful organisms, including Candida, Staphylococcus, Salmonella, Streptococcus, and E. coli. GSE and other plant-based remedies (except those refined into drugs) are capable of destroying only the *harmful* invaders of the body while leaving the helpful bacteria untouched. This modern "miracle" product is a must for every household.

> *Water Purification* - 6 to 30 drops per gallon of water will destroy pathogens, including giardia cysts.
>
> *"Tourista" prevention or cure* - 5 drops in a glass of water, used as a gargle, or swallowed.
>
> *Infections, Athlete's Foot* - 50 drops in 1 oz. of water, rubbed on the skin.
>
> *Diaper Rash* - 4-40 drops to 4 oz. water, depending on severity. Place in spray bottle and lightly mist the affected area at each diaper change for 4-5 days.

Cold Sores (Herpes Simplex 1)- 1 drop concentrate to 10 drops water, applied to affected area.

Canker Sores - 3 drops in 1/4 c. water or juice. Place in mouth and "swish" for 1-2 minutes. Repeat, if necessary.

Warts - Place a few drops on a bandaid and cover the wart. Repeat for up to 2 weeks.

Food Poisoning - 20-40 drops in water or juice (or use GSE tablets or capsules). Drink juice or take pills with 8 oz. purified water. One dose is usually all it takes!

Deodorant - 1 drop, diluted with enough water to spread under each arm. (Great for camping!)

Ear Ache - 4 drops in 1 T. vegetable glycerine. Heat a spoon in hot water or on a stove, fill with several drops of the mixture, and pour into affected ear 1-2 times daily. Use as often as needed.

Sore Throat - 20 drops (or two GSE tablets or capsules) in 6 oz. water or diluted juice. Gargle deep in the throat and spit out or swallow.

For information on the GSE drops, tablets or capsules, or to order, call 1-888-232-6706.

HERBS

In her "Herb Walk" video, LeArta Moulton gives 75-minutes of instruction on how to identify over 137 plants and herbs for their edible and medicinal uses. The video comes with a 100 page manual giving detailed references on plants and herbs identified in the video, plus a glossary of plant parts and information on how to plant, harvest, and use herbs. LeArta's "Nature's Medicine Chest" contains full color 4"x6" photos of medicinal, edible and poisonous plants with their uses and information printed on the back. These are excellent for field trips, camping, and survival in the outdoors. For information, or to order, call LM Publications at 1-800-Herbsetc.

HOMEOPATHY

"Would you like to know how to use inexpensive, effective, natural remedies that have no side effects? If so, **Homeopathic Medicine At Home** (by Panos and Heimlich) is for you. ...As overwhelming numbers of Americans lose faith in modern medicine, this is the right era for us to learn about this time-honored method of healing, whose preparations are obtained from animal, vegetable and mineral sources.

"As the image of penicillin is tarnished by the reality of allergic reactions, why not examine a homeopathic, safe remedy as an appropriate treatment for strep throat, colic, morning sickness, tension headaches and the need for habit-forming laxatives?" Robert S. Mendelsohn, M.D.

I resisted using homeopathic remedies for over 20 years because I thought the claims were just too good to be true. Since our 5 children had only two or three illnesses that required a visit to the doctor, I put off studying about homeopathy until I recognized that all of us had a few small problems that were bothersome, but not serious enough for a visit to the doctor. I was ecstatic to find a large selection of self-help homeopathic books in the library, each with clear explanations of the homeopathic approach to treating minor ailments and emergencies. I was even more ecstatic to find that the remedies actually worked!

In just a few short months, we have successfully treated minor illnesses, as well as almost completely eliminating allergic reactions to foods and inhalants. I even overcame my fear of the dentist! I now have a complete homeopathic first aid kit and several good suppliers.

Each ailment generally has a number of remedies, depending on the specific circumstances and severity. Choose one or more reference books to use a guide in choosing the proper remedy and putting together a first aid kit.

What ailments are homeopathic remedies effective in treating — without negative side effects?
Accidents, Injuries and First Aid
1. Emotional Shock, Trauma, Fright, Bad News
2. Bruising and Contused Wounds: Sprains and Strains

3. Cuts (Incised Wounds) and Abrasions: Scratches and Grazes
4-. Puncture Wounds
5. Splinters and Foreign Bodies
6. Lacerated Wounds
7. Bites and Stings
8. Burns
9. Broken and Cracked Bones
10. Surgery and Operations
11. Childbirth

Common Acute Ailments
1. Fevers
2. Colds
3. Sore Throats
4. Flu
5. Earache
6. Croup
7. Cough
8. Digestive Problems: Food Poisoning, Diarrhea, Colic, Constipation
9. Teething, Toothache and Gum Abscesses
10. Headaches
11. Parasites
12. Sunstroke

Recommended Reading:
The Authoritative Guide To Grapefruit Seed Extract, by Allan Sachs, D.C., C.C.N.
Homeopathic Medicine At Home, by Maesimund B. Panos, M.D. and Jane Heimlich
Homeopathy For Children, by Henrietta Wells, MCH.RSHom
The Complete Guide to Homeopathy, by Dr. Andrew Lockie and Dr. Nicola Geddes
Let Like Cure Like, by Vinton McCabe
Recommended Website:
http://elixirs.com, or *health@elixirs.com.*   Or, call Kathryn Jones, Health Counselor, at 1-800-390-9970.

PIONEER REMEDIES

My mother and grandmothers relied on home remedies for all but the most serious illnesses. The following are some of my favorites, and we have used them all to "doctor" our 5 children at home—without the need for prescription drugs:

Cough Medicine. 2 T. honey, 1 T. butter, juice of 1 lemon. Take 1 T. at a time. OR: Set a pan of water on the stove, over low heat. Place a towel over the head and lean over steaming pan. Breathe steam for 2 minutes.

Chest Congestion. Mustard plasters help break up congestion and make breathing easier. Mix 1 egg, 1 T. of dry mustard and 2 T. of oil. Thicken with flour, spread the mixture on a thin cloth and put this between a square of flannel or cotton. Apply it to the chest. Leave on for 10-20 minutes, repeating every 4 hours, as necessary.

Sore throat. Throat wraps have been effective in "curing" sore throats for generations. Apply medicated chest rub (with menthol) to the neck and throat area, then a cold, wet cotton cloth, covered with a larger dry cloth. (I often use an old cotton tube sock.)

(The theory behind this remedy is that the "heat" caused by the cold, wet cloth, as it comes in contact with the menthol, increases circulation which then brings more food nutrients and oxygen to the cells, carries away toxic wastes from dying cells, and increases the number of germ-devouring white corpuscles at the scene of the trouble, thereby promoting faster healing.)

Fever. The body's way of destroying bacteria, viruses and toxins is to elevate the temperature of the body. A fever signifies that something is out of order. A temperature of 103° in a child is the same as 102° in an adult. Go to bed and drink plenty of liquids (water with a little lemon juice added is best).

Sweat baths and Contrast baths (see below) will usually bring down a fever. For an accompanying headache, place an ice bag or cold compress on the head.

As long as the fever doesn't climb higher, it is important not to try to bring it down by using aspirin or other drugs. Allow the body to use the fever to heal.

Colds, Flu. Sweat baths help to eliminate toxins through the sweat glands. Lay down in a tub of hot water, about 98°F, and gradually add more hot water, to about 104° and above, until beads of sweat roll off the face. This usually takes 20-30 minutes. Drink water before and after the bath.

GENERAL PRACTICES TO HELP CLEANSE THE BODY

Contrast baths. Take sweat bath, as described above. Follow with a 1-minute cold shower. Wrap up in a sheet and lay in bed with plenty of covers to increase body temperature again. *(Both of these remedies again increase circulation to help the body heal more quickly.)*

Cleansing programs. It was a well known fact that after my grandparents went to a dinner party, they would go on a 3-day cleanse, usually eating nothing but fresh juices and a little raw fruit. The body cannot handle a steady supply of rich foods without becoming toxic.

Simple foods are best. After a vacation or food-filled holidays, your body would love to have a rest. If you find you are feeling a little "under the weather," give your body a break. For a few days, drink lots of fluids, and eat only fresh, raw fruits and vegetables.

HERBS TO GROW AND USE

My favorite herbs are inexpensive or easy to grow. We have used them to ease or relieve symptoms, often curing most common ailments and illnesses.

Aloe Vera

This plant is easy to grow indoors. The long, succulent leaves are cut open and a gel-like juice scraped out to be used to soothe and heal burns, stings, bites, and other minor skin irritations. We most often use this on sunburns.

Cayenne (Capsicum)

Grown in the form of hot red peppers most often used for seasoning, this herb should be in every herbal medicine cabinet. The ripe peppers are picked, dried and powdered. Freshly ground cayenne stores well. It has been used as a gargle to soothe and heal sore throats, as an internal body cleanser, and as a stimulant to help increase circulation. It is used in many herbal combinations because of its value as a catalyst. We place it on a bandage to speed healing of minor cuts.

Comfrey

This is my all-time favorite remedy for overnight relief in bruises and sprains. Internally it is used as a blood cleanser. The nickname "knit-bone" was given because of comfrey's ability to speed the healing of broken bones. We now know that the allantoin in comfrey speeds the healing process. It is easy to grow no matter where you live. This hardy plant is excellent as a spring tonic. It is easily started from root cuttings. Leaves may be used fresh, dried or frozen. In an almost fatal biking accident, my mother sustained a serious concussion, with major bruising and swelling in the face and head. My sister and father juiced comfrey for her to drink to help heal her internal injuries. She laid her face in a flat pan of comfrey paste to help relieve pain and reduce swelling. She had an amazingly speedy recovery.

Echinacea

Most often used as a blood cleanser for conditions such as eczema, acne, and boils. Also used to improve digestion.

Garlic

In Russia, garlic is sometimes called "Russian Penicillin." According to Allan South in **The Sense of Survival,** "it reportedly induces sweating, acts as a diuretic, cleanses the stomach, reduces blood pressure, aids in kidney and bladder functions, and is antiseptic. Garlic buds also make good poultices for snake and insect bites." For our children's occasional earaches, we placed a 1/2 t. of warmed garlic oil into the ear canal, then applied heat from a lamp, hot water bottle, or a warmed onion.

Lobelia

Commonly called "Asthma Weed," this annual herb is found throughout Canada and the U.S. It has been used as an expectorant, diaphoretic, antispasmodic, stimulant, and relaxant. It has been known to give almost instant relief from suffocating phlegm and mucus which has collected in the respiratory tract.

Your health is your choice
Take CHARGE of it and learn to enjoy life in better health.

STEP 11

GROWING, SPROUTING
AND HARVESTING

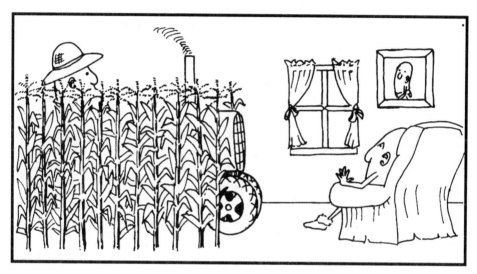

Nothing will bring a nation to its knees or into submission faster than a lack of food. If we are to be self-reliant, we MUST know how to produce our own food, using outdoor and indoor gardens. It doesn't matter if it costs more to produce a tomato in your own back yard than to purchase one from the grocery store! The knowledge and ability you gain to grow your own food is priceless. Some of my favorite teachers have stressed the importance of self-reliance when it comes to producing our own food:

"Plant gardens. Follow the counsel to have gardens wherever possible so we do not lose contact with the soil and so that we can have the security of being able to provide at least some of our food and necessities. Grow vegetables and eat those grown in your own yard. Even those residing in apartments or condominiums can generally grow a little food in pots and planters.

"Gardens promote independence.   Should the trucks fail to fill the shelves of the stores, many would go hungry. How do we evaluate the good that comes from the obvious lessons of planting, cultivating, and the eternal law of the harvest? And how do we measure the family togetherness and cooperating that must accompany successful canning?

"Yes, we are laying up resources in store, but perhaps the greater good is contained in the lessons of life we learn as we live providently and extend to our children their pioneer heritage." (**Teachings of Spencer W. Kimball**, p. 376)

Ezra Taft Benson, former Secretary of Agriculture, challenged us in 1974 to be self-sustaining through adequate preparation. *"An almost forgotten means of economic self-reliance is the home production of food. We are too accustomed to going to stores and purchasing what we need. By producing some of our food we reduce, to a great extent, the impact of inflation on our money."* (**Teachings of Ezra Taft Benson**, p. 265-266)

He spoke of the blessings of growing a garden, even a small one, to raise our own food. He said "Noah built his ark BEFORE the flood came, and he and his family survived. Those who waited to act until after the flood began were too late." He warned "The days ahead are sobering and challenging. ...Let us not be dissuaded from preparing because of a seeming prosperity today, or a so-called peace."

He also said "The revelation to store food may be as essential to our temporal salvation today as boarding the ark was to the people in the days of Noah." (*Ensign*, January, 1974.)

"We know that the Lord has decreed global calamities for the future and has warned and forewarned us to be prepared. For this reason, the Brethren have repeatedly stressed a "back to basics" program for temporal and spiritual welfare." (**Teachings of Ezra Taft Benson**, p. 267)

GARDENS

WHAT DOES IT TAKE TO GROW A GOOD GARDEN?

Gardening requires "know-how" and "do how." Knowing what to plant, where and how doesn't require much effort. Taking care of a garden that is properly planned and planted doesn't require much effort. It's just the DOing of it that keeps most people from getting started.

A good garden spot needs to be in the sun for at least half the day, close to water, fenced to keep out the big critters, and grown fertile soil. In most areas of the country, fertile soil is the toughest thing on the list because of all the chemical fertilizers and pesticides that have been applied to lawns and gardens. These products kill EVERYthing living. Earthworms and tiny "critters" can't replenish the nutrients in the soil and keep it "loose" so roots can travel freely. Compacted soil needs organic fertilizers, a generous supply of "mulch." a fresh supply of earthworms and composted kitchen food scraps.

Other good soil conditioners are rice or buckwheat hulls, peanut shells, coffee grounds, sawdust, peat moss, hay, straw, sand, and composted manure. You can even use feathers, cotton or wool clothing, leather coats, shoes and purses, as well as old newspapers. Bury it all and let the worms go to work on it! (It will take them a little longer to process these last items, so bury them where you won't be gardening for a year or so. The goal is to get a loose layer of dark soil at least 3" deep. You can tell if you have properly composted soil if it can be gathered up in your hand, pressed tightly, and it stays loose. If it forms a hard "clod," it still needs more conditioning.

We added sand and one bucket of earthworms to a "wormless" garden filled with heavy clay soil that would hardly grow weeds, and ended up with lush plants and worms in every shovel full of dirt. Even though earthworms produce approximately their own weight in fertilizer every day, it usually takes about 3 years to create a good organic garden with healthy plants that are virtually bug-free and very disease-resistant.

WHAT IF YOU HAVE A VERY SMALL GARDEN SPACE?

Learn to grow "up!" The vines of tomatoes, melons, and all legumes will cling to strings or poles or stakes (or even cornstalks), leaving the ground free for other crops.

NATURAL FERTILIZERS

Just like feeding the body properly is better than taking separate nutritional supplements, nourishing the soil will allow the soil to nourish your plants. What does the soil "eat?" Real food—just like we should be doing. It doesn't like animal products like meat scraps and fat—those just draw flies and grow maggots. (I would rather grow FOOD!) Adding fruit and vegetable scraps, green scungy things found growing in your refrigerator, stale or moldy bread, etc. helps nourish the soil.

You don't **have** to have a large compost area. You can just bury your kitchen garbage in the garden throughout the year. Within just a day or two, you will see the food begin to break down. Within a couple of weeks, you will see a healthy change in the color and composition of the soil.

We do have a round compost barrel mounted on a stand, with a handle for easy turning. This is perfect during the summer for disposing of grass clippings, but even that isn't necessary. (Using a mower that **does not** pick up the grass provides the lawn with all the mulch and nutrients it needs to grow...provided the lawn hasn't been treated with artificial fertilizers. For a healthy lawn, aerate it each year, "plant" some earthworms in several holes around the yard, and leave the clippings.)

Plant a winter "green manure" crop of wheat or rye grass, peas or other hardy green leafy plants towards the end of the growing season. Till it into the soil in the spring, to help maintain moisture, keep the soil loose, and add valuable nutrients to the soil for the following year's crops.

WHAT ABOUT BUGS?

Garden bugs are attracted to weak plants, so the healthier your plants are, the less they will be attacked...just like the human body! The safest, most effective pest control for any garden is to sprinkle diatomaceous earth on plants and surrounding soil throughout the growing season. When garden pests ingest this skeleton, the spiny parts in the diatomaceous earth tear up the intestinal tract.

As stated previously in the section on treating seeds for storage, diatomaceous earth is a white, powdery substance made up of the interior spiny skeleton of small marine creatures whose soft body parts have decomposed, leaving the remaining skeletons that accumulate on the ocean floor over thousands of years. These layers are then mined and used for pest control and filtering systems.

Our favorite "natural" liquid pesticide, especially good for aphids, is a mixture of 2 c. warm water, 2 cloves fresh minced garlic, 1 t. cayenne pepper, and 1 T. blackstrap molasses. Shake well and put into a spray bottle. Wet plants thoroughly. (I think the molasses attracts them, the pepper burns them, and the garlic suffocates them!!!)

Bird feeders and houses encourage birds to visit or live in your yard and feed from your garden. If you're very successful, though, you may have-to put netting over your prize tomatoes and other fruits, because they like those, too!

A favorite garden catalog containing "Environmentally Responsible Products That Work!"™ is Gardens Alive, 5100 Schenley Place, Lawrenceburg, IN 47025. Order from (812) 537-8650.

FAVORITE CROPS
Gardening in Oklahoma is a real challenge, so we tend to grow the "easy" things: green, yellow and red peppers, spinach, cucumbers, onions, peas, parsley and other herbs, tomatoes, lettuces, cabbage, comfrey, potatoes, beets, Jerusalem artichokes, melons, kohlrabi, and several varieties of green beans (I like the Japanese Long Bean because the beans grow to about 2 feet long in only 2 days!!).

For detailed organic gardening instructions, check out books and videos from your local library. Also recommended: **Skills For Survival**, by

Esther Dickey (includes information on saving your own seeds), and **The Sense of Survival**, by Allan South (includes companion planting guide, cold frame construction, and building a root cellar or storage pit).

SEEDS

It is important to collect seeds that can be used year after year. Most seeds are hybrids, and the seeds from what you harvest cannot be replanted to obtain the same plant. I remember hearing about the "Victory Gardens" grown during wartime when my mother was growing up. Jan Blum has created an "Independence Garden" plan which includes varieties of seeds with the most widespread adaptability and complete instructions.

These Garden PAKs and other non-hybrid seeds can be purchased from Seeds Blum, HC33, Idaho City Stage, Boise, ID 83706. Phone orders 1-800-528-3658; Customer Service 1-800-742-1423; e-mail 103374.157 @compuserve.com; website www.seedsblum.com. This is an excellent source for original seeds and valuable information on how to save your own seeds.

Check out the internet for other heritage, heirloom, or open-pollenated seed suppliers.

When buying regular seeds from local sources, check with your county extension service for varieties that grow best in your area. When I find a variety that grows well, I like to buy a 5-year supply and keep them tightly sealed and frozen.

TOOLS

A shovel is absolutely essential. Also helpful are a hoe, pitchfork, digging fork, buckets, hoses, wheelbarrow, stakes and cord for plants to climb up.

Black plastic is helpful to warm the ground for earlier planting and to place in between rows or over the entire garden, cutting holes for plants.

Sprouting

Because of our need for fresh "live" food and the enzymes and healing properties these foods contain, it is essential that a variety of sprouting seeds be an absolutely essential part of every home storage program.

DIRECTIONS FOR SPROUTING

Supplies needed:
- **Sprouting containers.** Use *wide mouth quart jars* for alfalfa and other small leafy greens; *trays* for beans and wheatgrass, as well as buckwheat or sunflower "lettuce."
- **Sprouting lids** (available at health food or preparedness stores), **fabric netting** or a piece of **fiberglass screen** to cover jar opening. (In dry climates, a piece of nylon stocking works well.)
- **Sprouting seeds.** Organically grown seeds sprout the best for me. Any seed capable of growing into a plant will sprout.

The chart below will give you approximate amounts to use and how long the sprouting process should take. Times vary depending on age of seed and room temperature.

Type	Amount	Soaking Time	Sprouting Time	Yield
Alfalfa, quinoa, clover, radish, cress, or cabbage	2 T.	4 hrs.	5-7 days	2 c.
Grains, beans, peas, lentils, pumpkin, or sunflower	1/2 c.	10-12 hrs.	2-3 days	1 1/2 c.
Mung or soy (long)	1 c.	10-12 hrs.	5-6 days	4 c.
Wheat (for grass)	1 c.	10-12 hrs.	5-6 days	3 c.
Sunflower, or buckwheat (for lettuce)	1 c.	10-12 hrs.	5-6 days	2 c.

Advance Preparation
- **BUY FRESH SEEDS.** Fresh seeds tend to sprout faster and germinate better than those stored for long periods of time. Fresh seeds of all types are usually always easy to sprout, especially if they are from the current year's crop. Older seeds, especially beans, are usually slow to sprout

and many in a batch will turn slimy and refuse to sprout. If you plan to buy large quantities of seeds for sprouting, ask for a sample and sprout a small amount first to test freshness. (If your stored beans or grains don't sprout, grind them to a flour and use them for thickening or baking, or cook them whole. If seeds taste bitter, they are too old. Toss 'em!)

❧ **ROTATE YOUR SEED STORAGE.** Using sprouts often and buying a fresh supply of sprouting seeds each year will ensure best results.

❧ **For long-term storage, "AERATE" STORED SEEDS EVERY YEAR.** Dry seeds are "alive," but dormant. They "breathe" at a very slow rate, giving off carbon dioxide, so they need fresh oxygen periodically. If you choose to store sprouting seeds only for use in emergencies, Connie Nielsen of Life Sprouts, recommends pouring seeds out of, and then back into, their storage containers once every year or two.

❧ **START FRESH SPROUTS OFTEN.** One of the best reasons to sprout is to be able to enjoy foods that are fresh and **full** of essential nutrients. Most seeds reach maturity after 2-5 days of sprouting. The vitamin C and enzyme levels begin to decrease after that time, so start small batches of sprouts often, rather than growing a huge batch and storing it in the refrigerator. I like to start a small amount of a different seed each day, in addition to my favorites that I sprout about twice a week. If I end up with too many sprouts to use raw, I freeze all but the green, leafy ones to use later in cooking.

Ready, Set, GO!

1. Sort and soak dry seeds. All seeds should be sorted, removing broken seeds and small pieces of debris. Place in a quart jar. Place sprouting lid or fabric (see suggestions above) over the top of the jar. If using fabric, secure with a jar ring or wide elastic band. Rinse seeds well, then pour off water and add soaking water—twice as much water as you have seeds. (Because of the excess salt in softened water, and the chlorine in city water, it is best to use purified water for soaking and rinsing.)

2. After soaking, pour off water and drain well. Whether you leave seeds in the jar or transfer to a tray, tipping the container slightly will help seeds drain better. Most failures at sprouting occur because seeds are not drained properly. (After soaking **beans,** pour onto sprouting tray and remove any seeds that have not expanded and are still hard; they will **not** sprout.) When no water drips from sprouts, roll jar so that most seeds coat sides of jar. To sprout in trays, spread seeds evenly, drain well, and cover with a lid or cloth to retain moisture and keep out light. Move to a warm (about 70°F) place and rinse with lukewarm water 2 times a day (or just often enough to keep moist, for small seeds like alfalfa) until sprouts have reached the desired length.

3.   **Harvesting.** Any seed CAN be eaten when the sprout has pushed through the outer shell of the seed. Most grains, beans and larger seeds are best when the sprout is as long as the seed. For instructions on growing "lettuce," wheat grass, and long, fat bean sprouts, see *Natural Meals in Minutes*, pp. 84-85.

4.   **"Greening."** When leaves have appeared on small seeds like alfalfa, and sprouts are about 1" long, place jar in a light place (not in direct sunlight) to "green" for 3-4 hours, allowing the chlorophyll to develop.

5.   **"De-hulling."** After "greening," put sprouts into a gallon jar or large pitcher and fill with water. The hulls will sink to the bottom or float to the top. Skim off floating hulls, then pour off water while lifting sprouts to top of the jar to allow water and hulls at the bottom of the container to pour off freely.

6.   **Storing Sprouts.** Like any fresh vegetable, nutrients in sprouts deteriorate as soon as the sprout has reached maturity, usually within 2-3 days. Rather than grow large quantities of sprouts to store in the refrigerator for a week or more, start small quantities of fresh sprouts every few days. Check sprouts carefully, and if any mold appears on any type of sprouts, do not eat.

Store sprouted seeds in a covered container with paper toweling on the bottom and between layers. Use within 4-5 days. Sprouted beans and grains can be frozen for later use. Mung and soy beans that are sprouted to about 2" long turn limp when thawed, but can still be used in cooking. I put 2-cup portions of sprouted grains or legumes in quart zip-loc bags, force out excess air, then stack flattened bags in the freezer where they store well for 1-2 months.

HOW TO GROW SPROUTS IN COLD WEATHER
Sprouts will still grow in cold weather, but germination will be slower. In case of a power outage, you can "incubate" them by setting them in their jars or trays inside a "cooler," with 1-2 covered jars of boiling water set in the center. Place lid on top. The water may need to be reheated one or more times each day. A heavy cardboard box wrapped in a mylar blanket, or covered with heavy foil, will also work well to provide a warmer sprouting environment.

POPULAR USES FOR SPROUTS
Since many vitamins, minerals, and enzymes are destroyed in cooking, try to use the tender raw sprouts in uncooked recipes whenever possible, or add to cooked foods just before serving. Use them in drinks and smoothies, omelets, meat loaves, patties, in bread dough, casseroles, stir-fry, salads, or as "lettuce" in sandwiches.

Harvesting and Preserving

Farmers and others have long used their ingenuity in finding ways to store vegetables from one harvest season to the other. Some of the methods they have devised would help us all in this matter of setting up a more adequate food storage program.

When my mother grew up, pits and cellars were common, with their sloping (and sliding) doors and various kinds of entrances. Some pits were entirely underground, some halfway, while others were above ground. Some were under the house, some by the house, and some out in the field. Above-ground "pits" were cone-shaped, or igloo-shaped mounds, covered with straw and soil. Celery and cabbage were stored in trenches.

BASEMENT STORAGE
If you can partition off a small room on the north or east side of the house, you can insulate it for storage. You need one or two windows for cooling and ventilating. Set up shelves. Removable slatted flooring facilitates air circulation. In dry climates, sprinkle water or wet sawdust on the floor to raise the humidity.

Crops can be stored in bins or wooden crates. Root crops also keep crisp in moist sand and in peat moss. Most crops store well in plastic bags with 1/4" holes cut in the sides for ventilation. Tie bags at top to keep in as much moisture as possible.

OUTSIDE STORAGE

In many parts of the country, vegetables can be left in the garden where they grew. One family near Portland, Oregon, where the average winter temperature is about 40°F, reports that out of ten years when they left crops in the ground, only two of those years were severe enough to ruin the vegetables. They planted late crops of cabbage and cauliflower that matured at different times during the winter.

If winters are severe, and you want to dig your vegetables and store them in PITS, etc., be sure to:
Stagger your planting so some crops mature late in the fall.
Leave them in the ground as long as possible.
Dig the vegetables when the soil is dry.
Cut plant tops 1/2" above the crown.
Wash vegetables, but dry them off before storing.
Protect them from drying winds.

For *storage places,* you can use:
A plastic or wooden barrel placed on its side and covered with straw and soil.
An old refrigerator buried in the ground with its door facing upwards.
Small cone-shaped outdoor mounds for storing potatoes, carrots, beets, turnips, parsnips, cabbage, or winter apples or pears.

DIRECTIONS:
1. Choose a well-drained location.
2. Make a nest of straw, leaves, or other bedding material on the ground.
3. Bury the vegetables (small quantities of different kinds), covering with more bedding.
4. Cover the mound with about 4" of soil and firm the soil with the back of the shovel.

5. Dig a shallow drainage ditch around the mound.

6. Allow for ventilation into the mound by having a small amount of the bedding material extend up through the soil to the top of the pile.

   Cover the opening with a board or with sheet metal to protect it from rain.

Note that pits or mounds should be in a different place every year, since leftovers in used pits usually are contaminated.

Large outdoor pits are not practical unless the winter temperatures in your area average 30° or below. If you use them, remember::
   —Dirt floors help maintain proper humidity.
   —Underground cellars maintain a more uniform temperature. (They also can serve as storm or fallout shelters.)
   —Members of a family or group in the same vicinity could share a large storage pit.

MISCELLANEOUS INFORMATION

The dampness of outdoor pits encourages decay and is not recommended for sweet potatoes, pumpkins and squash, onions, or peppers.

Sweet potatoes, pumpkins and squash should be stored in a dry place at 55° to 60°. For better keeping, harden the rinds and heal surface cuts by curing (by a heater or furnace) for 10 days at 80° to 85°. (Acorn squash is the exception — curing makes it stringy and orange-colored, whereas it should be dark green.)

Onions sprout and decay at high temperatures in high humidity. Store in open, loosely-woven bags at room temperature or slightly cooler.

Peppers (green) will keep for 2 or 3 weeks in a box with a polyethylene liner at 45° to 50°. (Make twelve to fifteen 1/4" holes in the liner.)

Late crop *potatoes* will keep for several months in a cool, dark place at 45° to 50° with good ventilation. Higher temperatures cause sprouting and shriveling. Lower temperatures may give potatoes a sweet taste. Light causes greening and lowers eating quality.

Apples keep best at about 32° where temperature remains the same and the air is rather moist. Do not store apples and vegetables together in the same place.

Leave *parsnips* in the ground. The flavor and texture improve with frost.

Pull *cabbage* up by the roots and place head down in a long mound, above ground level. Cover with straw and soil and dig a drainage ditch around the mound.

FREEZING

Freezing is a safe and easy way to preserve perishable foods, because bacteria can't grow in zero temperatures. Be sure to:
— Place packages of unfrozen food against the wall surface of your home freezer.
— Space packages apart.
— Keep the new packages away from food that is already frozen.
— Restrict the amount of food you are freezing to no more than 10% of the freezer capacity at any one time.

DIRECTIONS FOR FREEZING
String Beans
1. Wash whole tender beans and stem for 3 1/2 minutes, one pound at a time, in a wire basket above 2" of boiling water.
2. Chill in cold running water, then in ice water.
3. Pack in any size freezer zip-loc bags.
4. Flatten bag, forcing out air, and place in freezer.

Greens
1. Wash young tender leaves, discarding thick main stems.
2. Water scald (do not use the steam method). Put a pound of leaves in a wire basket or cheese cloth and immerse in 2 gallons of boiling water for 3 minutes.
3. Chill immediately as for beans, drain and package in freezer zip-loc bags, as above.

Eggs (Keep from nine months to a year.)
Use only fresh, clean, chilled eggs. Yolks and white can be frozen separately.
1. Stir yolks and whites with fork. Do not beat.
2. Pour into ice cube trays. (3 cubes = 2 large eggs)
3. Place in freezer.
4. When frozen solid, remove from trays and place in freezer zip-loc bags.

To use, thaw in refrigerator or place in a bag under cold running water. Use within 24 hours.

Fish
Glazing takes the place of zip-loc bags. A thin layer of ice seals the food, preventing air from getting to it. Whole fish, poultry, and game can all be glazed.
1. Freeze raw meat without wrapping or covering.
2. Dip quickly in ice water to form a thin film of ice over the product.
3. Repeat the water dip and freezing procedure until glaze is 1/8" thick.

DEHYDRATING

Dried foods take only a tenth as much space as bottled or canned foods. A bushel of dried peaches can be stored in a gallon jar. Surplus garden produce can be dried to use in soups, breads, and just to eat plain. You can blend dried vegetables for an instant soup mix. Add bouillon and water and you have instant soup! Powdered vegetables also make excellent baby food. Just add the powder to boiling water and simmer about 1 minute. Rather than give away the excess, dry it!

DRYING FOOD AT HOME   We marvel at new commercial methods of dehydrating food, but although there is currently a revival of interest in the home drying of foods we find very little written on home drying since World War II, when Victory garden surpluses made this a popular method of food preservation. Certainly in our effort to be self-sustaining we should know about one of the oldest and most natural methods of preserving food.

Advantages of Dried Food
— Nutritive values remain high.
— Dried food occupies only about one-fourth as much space as ordinary canned goods.
— Spoilage and rotation worries are reduced. There is no waste.
— New dried foods are helping to alleviate world hunger.
— Should you change homes, dried foods are easily transported.
— They are ideal for travelers, hikers, campers, rescue workers, etc. (Instead of carrying 16 fresh apricots with you, carry a pound of dried ones - 175 of them.)

THE DRYING PROCESS
Many apparently solid foods such as apples and potatoes are over 50%water. As the water is drawn out of them, the enzyme action (which spoils food) is suspended. Moisture and warmth are needed to start the enzymic action in full swing again.

In removing water from food, a combination of heat and warm moving air is best. We dry foods in the sun, in specially built dehydrators, or in the kitchen oven.

Heat from the sun. This is the most ancient method, and continues to be widely used. When Esther lived in the country, she spread out corn and apples on clean sheets or feed sacks and dried them on the roof of the wood shed or the flat bed of the hay rack. To complete the drying she strung apples in loops that hung from the clothes line.

In Thailand, she saw bananas drying in shallow bowls with a glass over the top to focus the sun's rays. The same principle is used when old windows are placed over food to dry it in the sun.

Specially built dehydrators. Dehydrators can be built of any size, any shape. Warm moving air dries the food on racks. A heating element provides the heat, allowing about 60 watts for each square foot of tray area. (150-watt light bulbs in porcelain sockets work fine.) A small 10" fan circulates air through the food to the top where the hot moist air escapes through a vent that can be regulated. A hole in the box near the bottom (opposite the fan) provides a fresh air intake. Between 15 and 20 hours are required to dry a 40-pound load of halved prunes or peaches, or a 20-pound load of sliced or shredded vegetables.

Oven drying. With the oven drying method it is difficult to control the temperature and moisture, but with experience it can be done. You should:
— Prop the door open to control heat and let out moist air.   (Gas oven, 8", electric oven, 1/2".)
— Check temperature with oven thermometer. (Do not use top unit in electric oven.)
— Aim at an even temperature of 150°. Too low a temperature will sour the food, while too high a temperature will harden it on the outside, thus preventing moisture inside from being released.
— Use trays made to fit the oven (wood frame with plastic screen, cotton netting, or wood slats tacked on). During World War II many people were using four trays that fitted in a rack in the oven. In this way about 10 pounds of fruit or vegetables could be dried at one time — more, if the vegetables were light-weight and leafy. (These same trays can be used to stand on the stove above the burners, or hang from the ceiling where the air is hot.)
— Don't overload the trays, since this prevents good air circulation. For sliced fruit and vegetables (light weight) use one pound per square foot of tray space. For heavy, halved fruit, use about two pounds.
— Alternate the trays so that food will dry evenly. Remove food from around edges as it dries.
— Keep trays 3" from oven floor. Mineral oil on wood frames prevents food from sticking.
— Store in deep freeze any food which is not completely dried but which you have to remove.

Apricots, peaches and pears: Treat as indicated below to prevent discoloration. Remove pits, slice in halves for drying (pit side up). Dry at 150°. Fruit should be pliable and leathery when dry.

Prunes: Dry in halves or whole. If drying them whole, first "check" skins (see below).

Apples: Peel, core and cut in 1/4" slices or rings. Treat for discoloration. Place 1 layer deep on trays. When dry, they will be creamy white, pliable and springy. (Note that the late variety, firm, mature fruit is best for drying.)

Berries: When drying blackberries, dewberries, loganberries, or raspberries, spread ripe, firm fruit in thin layers on drying trays (cloth under the fruit will prevent sticking). Set oven at 115°, gradually increase this to 150°, then gradually lower temperature during last stage of drying. Cherries can also be dried at low temperatures.

Vegetables: Beans (shell or snap), beets, broccoli, cabbage, carrots, celery, corn, onions, peas, peppers, potatoes, pumpkin, spinach, squash, and tomatoes, have been successfully dried. (Cut up combinations of dried vegetables in small pieces for soup mixes, or make a nutritious vegetable powder for soups by grinding dried leafy and other vegetables to a fine powder.) Note that:
— Vegetables should first be steamed in a wire basket above 2" of rapidly boiling water (cook until tender but firm). Test when cool, After drying they should be brittle, and should snap sharply when bent.
— Beans, peas, potatoes and spinach should be rinsed in cold water after being steamed.
— Most vegetables need to be steamed for 6 to 10 minutes. Exceptions are leafy greens and celery (3 to 4 minutes) and string beans and beets (15 to 30 minutes).
— Vegetables should be dried at temperatures ranging from a low of 115° to a high of 150° Start shell beans, peas, potatoes, and peppers at low, gradually increase to high, and reduce to low for last hour of drying. Start leafy vegetables on high and gradually reduce to low.
— Pumpkin or squash should be cut into strips 1" wide and about 1/4" thick. Peel, and remove seeds and pithy material. Steam until tender, about 6 to 8 minutes. Spread on trays 1/2" deep. Start drying at 150° to 160°, and cut temperatures to 120° during last hour. Change positions of drying trays often.

Meat and Fish: If you don't have a smokehouse to smoke meat, use your oven and dry it. To make jerky, remove fat and muscle from cheap cuts of beef shank, chuck, or venison. Cut in strips 1/4" thick and 1" wide, cutting along and not across the grain. Pound into the meat a seasoning of salt, pepper, oregano, marjoram, basil and thyme. Spread on wire racks in oven set at 120°, leaving door slightly open to permit moisture to escape. Turn over when half done. (It will take about 10 hours to dry.) Jerky is done when it is shriveled up and black, but it should be taken out of the oven when flexible enough to bend. It will get more brittle as it cools. (About 4 Ib. of fresh meat will make 1 lb. of jerky.)

Cut fresh salmon in strips 3/4" thick and cut squares 1 1/2" x 2 1/2". Soak in brine (1/4 cup salt to 1 qt. water) for one hour. Remove, sprinkle with salt and pepper, and brush with liquid smoke. Place on racks with air space between strips. Dry at 170° for 24 hours.

HASTENING DRYING, PRESERVING COLOR AND VITAMINS
With fruits, expose more of the surface of food to heat and air by pitting the apricots, quartering the pears, slicing the apples in rings, and peeling the peaches. Dip whole prunes, figs, and grapes in boiling water for 1 or 2 minutes to "check" skins, permitting moisture to escape.

Darkening of fruit occurs because certain chemicals within food unite with oxygen. To prevent this, you either:

— Dip fruit in salt-water bath of 4 to 6 tablespoons salt to 1 gallon water for about 10 minutes; or
— Precook fruit in steam or boiling water until it is tender but firm.

With vegetables, blanching or steaming them before drying helps preserve valuable vitamins, sets the color, and hastens drying by loosening the cell structure and tissues. It also ensures that the flavor will be better when the vegetables are cooked later. Keep vegetable pieces smaller than fruit. Shred, dice, or slice, keeping the pieces no thicker than a large pea (about 1/4").

MISCELLANEOUS DRYING IDEAS

You can dry sheets of food in the oven. Try making prune, banana or apple sauce "leather" by making a puree and spreading it thin on a teflon cookie sheet. Peel off when dry and pliable, like leather. Cut with scissors in small strips for snacks. Try a combination of fruits (grated apples with banana puree over the top, for example) and dry until crisp. Apricot and pineapple blended together is good. So is banana pureé, mixed with oatmeal or sesame seeds. Spread thin on a cookie sheet and dry to a crisp cracker. Try berries of all kinds mixed with sweet bananas.

SALTING AND BRINING

Salting and brining is a simple, inexpensive method and requires no special equipment, materials or skill. In many rural areas, or when it isn't feasible to freeze, dry or can, this method is used to preserve both meat and vegetables. And if the electricity supply were cut off for a considerable period, this method would be a good way to prevent the spoilage of food in the deep freeze.

VEGETABLES

Fermentation of vegetables is the same as salting and brining. Details for fermenting string beans are shown below. Other vegetables suitable for this treatment are:

Cabbage
Turnips
Corn
Vegetable greens
Peas and lima beans (unshelled)
Onions
Cucumbers
Carrots
Cauliflower
Green and red peppers
Beets

In the salting and brining of vegetables, bacteria feed on the sugars which are drawn from the vegetable material by the salt or brine. In the process, acid is produced.

GENERAL DIRECTIONS AND PRECAUTIONS

Use any clean containers but metal ones -- e.g., crocks, wooden barrels or kegs, glass fruit jars, or plastic buckets.

To keep the food pressed down in the containers use a cover of wood or a plate, or wooden cross pieces (from ice cream sticks) for glass jars. For a weight over the cover use a clean stone, paraffined brick, or a bottle filled with water.

As the curing proceeds, remove the scum which develops -- otherwise it will use up acid produced from fermentation.

FERMENTING VEGETABLES

Fermented food sounds like something you wouldn't want to eat. But it is delicious! A German lady's fermented string beans had been bottled for over two years but they were a fresh green color, crisp and sour, like pickles.

Vegetables processed by fermentation are preserved without heating. This factor would preserve enzymes, vitamins and minerals normally destroyed by the high temperatures necessary in other canning methods.

EQUIPMENT
Crock jar (five gallon)
Fruit jars (with glass lids)
Plate (or round hardwood board)
Weight (water in gallon jar)
Cotton cloth (two squares)

INGREDIENTS
Vegetables
Salt and water
Fresh dill or the seeds
Grape leaves
Garlic and pickling spice

The process for making fermented food is similar to making sauerkraut.

Put layers of vegetables, salt and spices in a crock and cover vegetables with grape leaves to preserve the color. Next, add a cloth, a plate and a weight. In ten days to two weeks it will be ready to put into bottles. Here is the process in detail:

1. Pick the string beans when they are small, just as the bean is beginning to form. (Older beans will be soft inside and tough outside.) Cut in 2" pieces. Weigh the beans.
2. Measure the water needed to fill the crock (about 6 to 7 quarts). Divide equally into two containers.
3. One-half cup of non-iodized salt (5 ounces) is needed for every 10 lb. of vegetables. Divide the required amount in equal parts and dissolve it in the two containers of water. (Water containing too little salt will make the beans soft instead of snappy crisp.)
4. In the bottom of the crock, place one bunch of fresh dill with seeds attached. (If this is not available, use the seeds from packages.)
5. Fill the crock with several layers of cut beans, and pour salt water over them. When the crock is nearly filled with beans, make a hole in the center and put in a handful of garlic (four or five whole garlic buds, each cut in two). Add one heaping tablespoon of pickling spice. Mix throughout the beans with a wooden spoon, or wash hands and arms and mix.
6. Put about four layers of overlapping grape leaves on top and cover the crock with a cotton cloth large enough to hang down over the edge of the crock for a few inches all around.
7. Over the cloth put an inverted plate, or a round hardwood board a little smaller than the crock. Weight it down with a gallon jar containing as much water as needed. Cover with a clean cloth to keep away gnats, etc.
8. When foam starts building up, skim it off carefully for about four or five days. A greyish or brownish scum comes up on the plate and cloth and if this is not removed it will destroy the fermentation acid and the beans will be soft. To remove scum, remove the weight and plate. Fold the cloth to the center, take it to the sink, wash it out, and replace cloth, plate and weight.
9. Shake the crock. If you hear no bubbling, the fermentation is complete. (It should take from 10 days to 2 weeks, depending on the temperature.)

The beans are now ready to put in bottles. *When taking them out of the crock or jars, use a fork or a spoon, not the fingers, as you may start a new fermentation.* Use glass lids if available, or plastic wrap and a metal canning ring. Fill jars to the very top with beans and with the juice from the crock, so that there is no room for air. Put them in a cool place on layers of paper so that any juice leaking out won't damage the shelf.

The beans are delicious with meat instead of pickles, or on sandwiches.

SAUERKRAUT

To make sauerkraut, it will take 25 or 30 lb. of cabbage for a 5-gallon crock. Use 1/2 cup of salt for every 10 lb. of grated cabbage. Put dill (optional) in the bottom of the crock, then layers of about 5 lb. of cabbage and one-fourth cup of salt. Repeat until crock is half full. Put in the garlic (optional), as in the directions for fermenting beans, and finish filling the crock. Put on the inverted plate and weight . Follow directions for keeping the scum off, as with beans. Fermenting has stopped when the small bubbles cease coming to the top. Then, put the sauerkraut in bottles, using the juice in the crock to fill to within 1/2" of the top. (If there is not enough liquid from the kraut itself, finish filling the jars with a salt solution, using 2 tablespoons salt to 1 quart water.)

If the storage place is warm and damp it will be necessary to process the sauerkraut and the beans after the fermenting period. Process in a hot water bath with water at least an inch over the top of the jars. For quart jars, process 30 minutes after the water begins to boil.

Fermentation of cabbage takes place best at about 60° to 65°. To achieve this it may be necessary to immerse the stone jar in a tub of cold water which you replace daily.

SALTING FISH

I like the idea of not being dependent on electricity to keep everything from spoiling. When the electricity goes off for days, due to damage done by storms or other weather-related problems, we often have to scramble to take care of food in refrigerators and freezers. While pressure bottling of meats over an open fire is an option, I am happy to have a second option that requires far less effort.

BRINING PROCEDURES FOR PICKLING FISH
1. Clean fish thoroughly.
2. Soak fish in weak brine made of 1 cup salt to each gallon cold water for 1 hour. Drain.
3. Make saturated brine of 4 cups salt to each gallon cold water. Soak the fish in saturated brine for 12 hours in a refrigerator (approximately 40°F). Soak small fish, like smelt, for 4 hours.
4. Rinse fish in fresh water.
5. Cut fish into serving size pieces.

Michigan State University Extension
Preserving Food Safely - 01600586 10/13/97

SALTING FISH
Salting is an ancient procedure for preserving fish that was introduced to the Great Lakes area by northern European immigrants. Salted fish was commonly consumed by travelers during the summer.

Salt preserves fish by removing water from the flesh and tying up the remaining water so that spoilage organisms cannot use it for growth. If enough salt is used, the fish may keep for as long as a year in a cool, dry place. Salting is one way to store fish until you are ready to smoke or pickle them.

If you are salting less than 50 pounds of fish, you will need no special equipment, just a sharp knife and a 2- to 4-gallon nonmetal container, a stone crock, or a wooden or food-grade plastic tub with a lid.

Salt should be pure and clean. Iodized table salt is not recommended. Use a high-purity pickling or canning salt available at many grocery stores.

Salt brine penetrates lean fish better than oily fish. Oily fish become rancid more readily than lean fish. However, oily fish can be excellent when salted.

DRY SALTED FISH

Fill a dish pan or shallow box with dry salt. Sprinkle a thin layer of salt on the bottom of the brining container. Dredge each piece of fish in salt, then place skin-side down in the container. Place large pieces with the backbone next to the container wall. An extra piece may be placed in the middle to level each layer. Overlap pieces as little as possible.

Pack small fish in a ring with tips of heads touching container walls. You may need to put one or two fish across the center to keep the layer level. Stagger successive layers so that each fish rests on two fish in the layer below.

Scatter a thin coat of salt between each layer. Pack the top layer of fish, both large and small pieces, skin-side up. The amount of salt used depends on the season of the year, fish size and length of preservation desired. A general rule is to use one part salt to three parts fish.

FRESHENING SALTED FISH

Salted fish can be smoked, pickled or used in a variety of recipes, but they need to be freshened in cold water first. Soaking in several changes of cold water for 8 to 48 hours (according to taste), in the refrigerator, should be sufficient. Should further freshening be desired, put fish in cold water to cover and just bring to a boil, then simmer. Cookery methods suitable for salt fish include broiling, frying, baking in milk or cream, simmering and creaming.

STEP 12

EMERGENCY PLANS & 72-HOUR KITS

Developing an **Emergency Action Plan** doesn't cost anything, and it is guaranteed to provide a feeling of peace. Some things to think about are... What kind of natural disasters occur in your area? In our area, we prepare for tornadoes. In other areas, it is flooding or hurricanes or earthquakes. You need to plan what you will DO if you are caught in the middle of severe weather? What about man-made disasters? Where will you go to be safe?

James Stevens, author of **Making the Best of Basics**, says "There are no emergencies for those who are truly prepared." Few people fall into the "truly prepared" category, including my family. Most of us don't have the opportunity to be *totally* self-sufficient. I'm satisfied if I am prepared enough just to keep emergencies from turning into disasters. The way we handle a situation often determines the severity of the outcome.

HAVE A FAMILY COUNCIL

In family councils or preparedness meetings, some families have designated meeting places where each member of the family is to go if an emergency has threatened their home. In the event of nationwide disaster, they have made plans for meeting with family members living away from home. Whether you're making big plans or small ones, it takes some time and effort to make your PLAN. Consider what disasters are likely to happen, decide what you can do to keep your family and friends together, and to create order out of chaos. Assign responsibilities, establish accountability, rehearse your plan, then put it on paper so it can be reviewed frequently.

You have all heard how to "drop and roll" in the event of a fire in your home, but have you taken the time to role play so all family members can be familiar with the procedures? Why not stage "fire drills" for all kinds of emergencies? A group of interested families are currently making a "game" out of living on their food storage for at least a week (no trips to the store or "out" to eat), using it as an opportunity to see how prepared they really are. Practice runs will help everyone feel more comfortable if and when the drill becomes a reality.

Working with church or neighborhood groups, people can help each other be prepared to DEAL with any emergency in a calm, *orderly* manner. The following plan is used by some members of the Church of Jesus Christ of Latter-day Saints:

EMERGENCY PREPAREDNESS PLAN

OBJECTIVES: Individual awareness and involvement
                     Every family prepared to handle any emergency
1. 72-hour kit for each person
2. A minimum of a 2 month supply of food, fuel (where possible) and clothing in each household, preferably enough for 1-2 years (2-week supply of water).
3. Family emergency preparedness plan with each member trained to follow the plan. Each member also trained in first aid and CPR.

4. Neighborhood group plan: In a disaster situation the neighborhood leader checks each family in his group and reports status and needs to priesthood leaders or to the ward Emergency Preparedness (EP) Specialist.
5. In the event of a disaster, the EP specialist and Bishop's counselor coordinate relief within the ward using Relief Society and Priesthood leaders.
6. To implement: Use ward newsletters and bulletins to urge preparedness and home storage. Teach cooking classes. Also use ward EP fairs, and Relief Society homemaking meetings to teach basic self-sufficiency skills.
7. Involvement:
   A. Every family actively involved with neighborhood group.
   B. Home Teachers actively involved in EP awareness.
   C. Relief Society actively involved in training family members or neighborhood groups in the plan, first aid skills, storing and using basic foods.
   D. The bishop is ultimately responsible, but should delegate the training and implementation of the plan to his counselor who will work closely with the EP specialist and the ward welfare committee,

OVERALL PLAN

Be prepared to meet the needs of its members by drawing upon resources of the ward members, as indicated in the Preparedness Survey that follows.

Preparedness Survey

Ward or Group _____ Home Phone _____

Date _____ Bus _____

Name _____

Home Address _____

Business Address _____

Training and Skills

1. Medical: Specialty _____
   Instructor capabilities: Yes__ No__   Certification: Yes __ No __
2. Construction: Specialty (plumber, electrician, carpenter, etc) and skill (professional, hobby, retired) _____
3. Heavy equipment operator: _____
4. Mechanical: Diesel, auto, air conditioning, heating, or other_____
   _____
5. Communication: List amateur radio, commercial experience and equipment you have. _____
6. Group cooking: Experienced in preparing large group meals.
   Yes __ No __
7. Other skills or talents: _____

8. Additional language spoken _____
   Fluent Yes __ No __   Spoken: Regularly __ Occasionally __

Physical Health

1. Family has current immunizations: Yes __ No__
2. Does your family exercise regularly (3-5 times per week)?
   Yes __   No __   Sometimes __
3. Is all the family trained in CPR?   Yes __ No __
4. In case of a major disaster, is there anyone in your home with special problems or needs who would need immediate care?
   (Please explain) _____
   _____
   _____
   _____

5. Do any family members need "Med Alert" tags but do not have them?
   Yes __ No __

Home Production and Storage

1. Do you have a garden?   Yes __ No __
2. Do you have fruit trees?   Yes __ No __
3. Skills in: Canning __ Drying __ Freezing __

4. Do you know how to compute a year's supply of food for your family? Yes __ No __
5. How much family food storage do you have? No comment __
      1-2 mo. __ 3-5 mo. __ 6-8 mo. __ 9-11 mo. __ more?__
6. Do you have two weeks of water stored? Yes __ No __
7. Do you have a year's supply of clothing? Yes __ No __
8. Do you have a sewing machine? Treadle __ Electric __
9. Do you have: Bread mixer   Hand __ Electric __
                        Wheat grinder Hand __ Electric __

Other Equipment and Skills

1. 72 hour kit for each person in family? Yes __ No __
2. First aid kit Yes __ No __
3. Water well Yes __ No __
4. AM/FM radio with batteries Yes __ No __
5. CB radio Yes __ No __
      Portable ___ Mobile ___
6. Fire extinguisher Yes __ No __
7. Trained shelter manager Yes __ No __
8. Do you have: 4-wheel drive vehicle, camper, pickup truck, heavy equipment, or riding horses? _____

_____

9. Do you have: chain saw, electric generator, air compressor, water pump, tent? _____

Secondary Heating Source

1. Do you have an alternate heating source if you lose primary heat?
                                                Yes __ No __
2. What type of heating system? _____
3. How long can you operate on the fuel supply on hand?
                              weeks _____ month(s) _____
4. Can all family members operate the alternate system? Yes __ No __

Other Emergency Information

1. Do members of your family know about the Emergency Broadcast System? (Information and instructions will be given on all AM radio systems) Yes __ No __

2. With serious damage to your home, secondary damage of fire, electrical shorts, or water leaks could do more damage. Are family members trained to turn off all utilities? Yes __ No __

3. If you are gone, do you have a plan with your neighbors to take care of each others homes? Yes __ No __

4. Do you have a wrench available at or near the gas meter to turn off the valve? Yes __ No __

5. Have you sent duplicate copies of all critical family records to a family member or trusted friend in another city? (Wills, titles, contracts, insurance policies, serial numbers of valuable property, photographs of possessions, inventories, etc.) Yes __ No __

6. Have you established family plans and do you practice them regularly for:
   A. Fire   Yes __ No __
   B. Earthquake   Yes __ No __
   C. National emergency   Yes __ No __
   D. An event that separates family members? Yes __ No __

Adapted from "Preparedness Assistance Packet", Compiled by Gary Clayton, former member County Sheriff's Dept., Provo, Utah.

EMERGENCY COMMUNICATIONS

In some situations, the ability to receive and send information may mean the difference between peace and panic, or even life and death.

In addition to a small portable AM-FM radio(at least one per family), it is important to have or have access to a short wave setup. Through short wave reception, you can gain access to information all over the world.

TEMPORARY EMERGENCIES

WHY PREPARE A 72 HOUR SURVIVAL KIT?
What will you do if disaster strikes your neighborhood: fire, riot, flood, tornado, hurricane, or earthquake? During the critical first 72 hours until relief efforts can be organized, YOU AND YOUR FAMILY MAY WELL BE ON YOUR OWN!

With very little expense and very little effort, it is possible to bring together a few basic items which will make a difficult situation less stressful, and may even save lives.

There are both physical and emotional effects that occur as a result of being placed in an emergency situation:
   1 - Emotional shock and often hysteria. Some people will "rise to the occasion," and others will fall apart or retreat into a protective shell. Preparedness training and overall peace of mind that God is in control of the situation help to lessen the severity of negative responses.
   2 - The likelihood of accidents increases. If panic sets in, thinking and reasoning are affected. People often act without thinking of the consequences, placing themselves and others in danger.

The greatest threat to life is accidents that lead to severe bleeding or other forms of injury or trauma. Knowing how to deal with these situations may well save lives. Any training you can get will be helpful.

72 HOUR EMERGENCY SUPPLY KITS

The first 72 hours are the most critical ones in a natural disaster. In case of an auto accident, a 72-hour car kit with an emergency first aid kit or food, light, heat and water may well be a life-saver. The idea is to have supplies gathered in one convenient bag that you can pick up and run with. What does one put into such a kit?

There is a difference in SURVIVING and living comfortably. If you have the money and the strength to carry a LARGE pack with all the "extras" in it, by all means do so, but it isn't necessary.

We can all survive on next to nothing if we have water to drink and are not too cold or not too hot, and I really like food, so I consider that as essential. Whatever I put into a pack is a luxury. If I am fortunate enough to have my kit with me in an away-from-home emergency , I will be thankful for everything in it.

IDEAS FOR FOOD IN 72 HOUR KITS

Choose high-calorie nutritious foods your family will enjoy. This is a good time for "treat foods" like granola bars, trail mixes, jerky, etc.

Rotate the food in your packs so you do not find yourself in an emergency situation with rancid or spoiled food.

Use only foods that are easy to prepare or ready to eat. If you're actually using this kit, it will be because you are away from your home, probably in a car or on foot. Do not plan to have all the luxuries of home. Cooking will most likely be difficult or impossible. In a pinch, you can learn how to be inventive and make the best use of whatever resources are available. It's amazing what we can accomplish when we have to, especially when we recognize that we can rely on inspiration from a loving Heavenly Father. We *won't* be left alone and without guidance!

WHAT GOES INTO A 72 HOUR SURVIVAL KIT?

First, you need a backpack or other container that can be easily carried. Large duffel bags and plastic buckets or other bulky containers may be handy for home use, but not when you're "on the go." Look for a sturdy backpack or small duffel bag with straps that will fit comfortably over the shoulders. Keep your hands free to carry other things. For small children, you might want to invest in a good wagon or portable luggage carrier so one person can carry several packs.

Don't store all your kits in one place. What if a fire was burning in the part of the home where they are stored? We store several inside and several in the garage.

Make sure to include ID tags on the outside of your kits. Include name, address and phone number, contact number for relative or close friend, and birth date.

KEEP 72-HOUR KITS SIMPLE!!

Essentials Of Home Production & Storage, published by the Church of Jesus Christ of Latter-day Saints, advocates putting together some easy-to-assemble articles when making up an individual 72-hour kit:

Food
3-day supply - about 1500 calories per day with essential nutrients.

Consider MRE's, beef or gluten jerky, packaged nuts, dried fruit, applesauce or fruit cups, aseptic containers of fruit or vegetables juices, trail mix, granola bars, or energy bars made of 1 c. ea, peanut butter, powdered milk, honey, raisins or dates, and raw sunflower seeds (see recipe section).

I love fresh, raw foods, so I store 1 c. each wheat, quinoa and lentils, for sprouting, in a zip-loc bag. On the 2nd day of any emergency, I will have live food to eat!

Water
2 qt./person (for drinking only) in 1 quart containers
Water Purification Drops and Disinfectant (NutriBiotic)

Bedding
Space Blanket or Wool Blanket
Lg. plastic Garbage Bag or Plastic Sheeting

Clothing
One change Outerwear
Two changes Socks and Underwear

Personal Supplies and Medication
Toiletries
Feminine Hygiene Supplies
Chapstick
Sun block
1 roll Toilet Tissue
Zip-loc Bags (qt. and gal.)
30-gal Garbage Bags and Ties
12 large paper Lunch Sacks
HandiWipes or Washcloth
First Aid supplies
Cleaning supplies
Extra pair Glasses (if you wear them), or Magnifier Sheet

Heat, Fuel and Light
Light sticks
Matches (waterproof container)
Long life Candles
Battery-powered light
Extra Batteries
Heat Packs (hand warmers) or Hot Water Bottle
Bic Lighter

Equipment
Emergency Handbook (covering first aid, signaling, etc. A boy scout handbook works well.)
Ear Plugs
Can Opener
Dishpan
Dishes or Mess Kit (or paper plates and cups)
Utensils
Drinking Cup
Radio (battery-powered) (in double zip-loc bags for water protection)
Paper
Pen
Whistle
"Fun Stuff" (crayons, coloring books, crossword puzzles, books to read)
Pocket or Utility knife
Heavy gloves (opt.)

Infant Needs (opt.)
Diapers
Sturdy Clothing
Formula
Cleaning Supplies

Personal Documents
Scriptures
Family records and legal documents

Money
$20 in cash

WHY BOTHER ?

Why have 72-hour kits? It is likely that you won't have to use them. But for such a small amount of effort, the peace of mind that results from knowing that you are prepared will allow you to be comforted, and that you need not live in FEAR!

What are "insurance policies" like this for if not to provide a little security and the likelihood that your basic needs will be met.

The following provides a brief summary of my reasons for including some of the items in my kit:

BATTERY POWERED RADIO
Local stations and the Emergency Broadcast System will be the only source of reliable information during an emergency. Check it at least every 6 months to make sure both it and the batteries are in working

order. Daylight Savings Time changes are good "reminder" events to change batteries and rotate food.

FAMILY RECORDS AND VALUABLES
Replacing Birth Certificates, Naturalization Papers, Diplomas, Insurance Certificates, Genealogy Information, Computer Disks, Passports, etc., would be a monumental task if all your originals to identify you as you were destroyed.

"FUN STUFF"
After the first few hours of an emergency, the changes in life style and circumstances can cause a great deal of emotional stress and an overwhelming feeling of insecurity, especially in small children and older adults. Items that are will divert attention from the situation at hand should be included in the emergency kit.

These can include crayons, coloring books, story books, puzzles, paper dolls, soft small toys for children. For adults, include books, handiwork, musical instrument, or some type of sports equipment to encourage physical activity.

PLASTIC BAGS AND TIES
Besides serving as garbage containers, plastic bags make excellent ground cloths, sleeping bag covers, tents, wash basins, and substitute rain coats.

DISINFECTANT
NutriBiotic Citricidal Liquid Concentrate can be used to treat sewage, drinking water, waste water, and refuse to destroy all bacteria and heal infections.

PORTABLE TOILET
Include a pointed shovel. Assemble 3 paper bags, one inside the other. Place in plastic bucket and fold the bags over the outside edge. (The size depends on how carefully you aim!) Twist or fold tops of bags after using, and bury in a hole at least 8" deep. Don't forget toilet paper!

DISPOSABLE PLATES, BOWLS , CUPS AND UTENSILS
If you don't have a "mess kit," disposable items are great. They will also help to conserve water.

SOAP
Waterless hand cleaner or liquid soft soap works best when water supplies are limited. Packaged moist towelettes are also excellent.

TOILETRIES
These are not essential for survival, but I'd like to be able to keep clean, and at least slightly well-groomed. Feeling "grungy" destroys my sense of well-being and makes me less likely to deal with a tough situation.

Plan on having at least a toothbrush, dental floss, toothpaste, comb or brush, washcloth and towel, deodorant, shaving supplies and mirror, shampoo, chapstick and possibly a small make-up kit.

FIRST AID
We can assume that major medical needs will be taken care of by community resources. Every community has a plan to dispatch paramedics, fire departments, police, and other medical personnel as needed to areas where major injuries have occurred.

The purpose, therefore, of the items included in the family First Aid Kit is to treat minor injuries so that they do not become a major threat to health during the first few days of an emergency.

Now is the time to enroll in some basic emergency medical training through your local Red Cross Chapter or community college. In only one day, you can become certified to administer CPR.

NutriBiotic Citricidal Grapefruit Seed Extract is effective at destroying bacteria and viruses, virtually eliminating the threat of infections. It provides a safe solution for illness related to contaminated food, water, and even from contact with human or animal waste! This "first aid kit in a bottle" is a must!

WATER STORAGE
Store a minimum of 1 gallon per person per day, preferably in 1 quart or smaller containers. What if you need more water? A 2-oz bottle of NutriBiotic Citricidal will treat up to 125 gallons of contaminated water.

SLEEPING BAGS and BEDROLLS
Wool blankets resist fire, they warm even when wet and they are less bulky than sleeping bags. Each person needs to be able to keep warm and dry.

EAR PLUGS
In case of tornadoes, hurricanes, flooding, or other circumstances when people are confined to a shelter, there are most often many people weeping and moaning at their losses, and usually a great deal of activity throughout the night. Ear plugs help block out a majority of the noise so you can get the best sleep possible.

CAN OPENER
A manual type must be packed with any canned goods. I like the heavy-duty Swingaway® brand.

UTILITY KNIFE
A sharp versatile knife, such as the stainless steel Leatherman or Coleman tools will give you pliers, wire cutters, a screwdriver, a saw, and scissors on some models.

HOT WATER BOTTLE
I get great comfort out of knowing that if I have a way to heat water, I will have warm hands and feet. The heat from one small water bottle is enough to provide warmth tootsies for hours!

EMERGENCY LIGHTING
FLASHLIGHT (Two battery)
 New batteries should last for up to 7 continuous hours.

CANDLES (Burning time)
3/4 diameter x 4" tall - 2 hrs.
7/8 diameter x 4" tall - 5 hrs.
2" diameter x 9" tall - 7 hrs. per inch
9" - 63 hours

LIGHT STICKS
Usually last for up to 8 hours. These provide very little light, but are good as a "beacon" or signal light from a short distance.

UTILITY SHUTOFF
ADJUSTABLE WRENCH - Keep this close to gas and water lines. Each member of the family should be trained how to turn off gas or water in the event of an emergency. If there are breaks in water lines, this may well prevent damage to one's home, and provide increased water pressure for community use.

In the event that you are without water, but still in your home, remember that water trapped in the hot water tank and indoor plumbing will stay clean once the main water valve is turned off.

CAR KITS
There are many instances when you could be stranded in your car, or forced to flee in your car. If you don't have room or funds for a complete 72-hour Car Kit, the following items would make any time spent in the car more comfortable:

1. First Aid Kit
2. Money
3. Flashlight with fresh batteries
4. Food (granola bars, nuts, raisins, fruit roll-ups, etc.)
5. Water
6. Large heavy trash bags for rain ponchos, ground cloths
7. Blanket
8. Fix-it supplies - duct tape, string, wire, tools
9. Car care items - tools, jumper cables, tow rope, flares
10. Entertainment - games, books, paper and pens

CHAPTER 4

LEARNING AND SHARING NEW SKILLS

Learning new information, then teaching others is what life is all about. Parents learn, then teach their children. Often children learn, then teach their parents. Only by gaining and sharing knowledge can we progress rapidly.

Once you understand the principles and techniques taught in this book, please share with others. The following methods of passing on information are ones I've been involved in over the last 30 years. It is my hope that you will share with others the responsibility of getting prepared. It is much more fun when you get a group together to organize the searching, researching, shopping, bargaining, teaching and training.

If you'd like to share your successes in teaching and training, please send them via e-mail to info@naturalmeals.com.

TEACHING AND TRAINING

ONE YEAR PROGRAM
TO TEACH PREPAREDNESS SKILLS

	Topic for Family Home Evening	Storage Item or How-To Information
JAN	Affordable Way To Store Food Inventory goods and set goals	Water Storage and Treatment
FEB	Family Emergency Response Plan	72 hr. Kit & Car Kit
MAR	Home Production and Gardens	Seeds - Sprouting & Storing
APR	Emotional Preparedness	Dry Beans (Legumes) FAST ways to use old or new beans
MAY	Fun and Games -Be Prepared to Have Fun!	Dried Milk - How To Use In Making Cheeses
JUN	Financial Preparedness	Clothing & Bedding
JUL	Neighborhood Groups	Bottling & Dehydrating supplies Canning and Food Preservation
AUG	First Aid Kits	Wheat & Other Grains Making Gluten (Meat Substitute)
SEPT	Home Repairs & Utility Turn Off's	Spices, Seasonings, Baking Supplies
OCT	Communication, Batteries, Radios	Rolled Grains, Pasta
NOV	Alternative Heating	Fuel, lamps, candles, flashlights and bulbs
DEC	Spiritual Preparedness and Goal Evaluation	Fats - oils, nuts and nut butters

PREPAREDNESS FAIR IDEAS

1. Design a program around the needs of your ward or group.
   a. Take into account the age groups and finances
   b. Keep it simple and plan to have one or two fairs each year, rather than one that is so comprehensive that people will surely feel overwhelmed.
   c. Participation is essential. The more people you involve in teaching, the more people will be prepared.
   d. Encourage members to learn new skills and then share them at the fair. Often, beginners are the best teachers. They don't overwhelm others with their vast knowledge.
   e. Encourage families (not just individuals) to give presentations.
   f. Include information and activities for children, if appropriate.
   g. Stage earthquake and other "what if" drills.
   h. Serve samples of meals made from nutritious stored foods. There is nothing like a taste of a yummy soup, bread, or dessert to give people confidence to use store foods regularly.
   (Note: There's nothing like the smell of home-baked bread and a bubbly pot of chili to spark an interest in using stored foods!)

2. Take advantage of the many resources in your area:
   a. Scouts, Red Cross and Individuals will come to provide training to groups.
   b. Utility companies will come to explain the dangers involved in any disaster and how to avoid them.
   c. Companies providing equipment and services are most often willing to come and demonstrate their wares, and give lectures and free information handouts for your home library.

3. Provide signup sheets for regular classes that would provide more extensive training, based on the topics highlighted at the fair.

4. Provide signup sheets for "experts" who attend the Fair to volunteer to share their knowledge in upcoming training sessions.

FOOD STORAGE COOKING CLASSES

Learning why nutritious whole foods are important and how to to cook with them is essential. Cooking is no longer taught in most homes or schools. With the advent of "fast foods," we have lost the "need" to cook from basic foods. The health benefits of returning to such meals and the peace of mind from knowing you have supplies on hand to make those meals are reason enough to learn how - NOW!

Cooking Class Outline
SHARING RESOURCES

JANUARY
Shopping Tips-How to choose foods without harmful preservatives and additives (from **The Food Storage Bible** by Benkendorf)
WHY we need to use basic foods on a daily basis- Nutrition and Enzymes/Antioxidants (from **Food Combining** by Bingham)
How to Afford a Year's Supply—one recipe at a time

FEBRUARY
Basic Equipment
Grinding and Cracking grains and beans
Quick Breads
Making your own Mixes

MARCH
3-Minute Bean, Pea and Lentil Soups, Sauces and Gravies
5-Minute Bean Dips

APRIL
Yeast Breads & Oil Pie Crusts

MAY
Sprouting, Gardening

JUNE
Sandwich Fillings, Meatless Patties

JULY
Smoothies, Healthy Snacks

AUGUST
Harvesting: Dehydrating, Freezing
Seasoning Mixes
Homemade Salad Dressings, Mayonnaise

SEPTEMBER
Home Canning & Using a Pressure Cooker

OCTOBER
Gluten - "Hamburger", "Meat"balls, Jerky

NOVEMBER
Hearty 15-minute soups from beans and grains
3-Minute Powdered Milk Cheeses

DECEMBER
Healthy Holiday Favorites

Joining or forming *Buying Clubs and Co-ops* is an excellent way to purchase large quantities of food and other supplies at a discount. In an organized group, responsibilities for finding the best buys can be shared.

Someone with a business license can usually get better prices on quantities of books and equipment. One person can search out the best prices on beans, another on honey, another on storage containers. Work with other groups to be able to purchase a truckload at a time for best bargains.

Set up a *Bargain Hotline* of those interested in passing on any special bargains they find. See p. 29 for detailed information.

Cooking Classes for beginners, by beginners! If you're not comfortable with teaching cooking classes, but could gather others together in a cooking classroom setting, you can use the Quick Wholesome Foods video to do the teaching for you. The video is divided into five 15-minute cooking segments covering 100% whole wheat breads, gluten ("meat" made from wheat flour), grains, beans, and powdered milk.

Using the recipe booklet included with each video, one person in the group can volunteer to do a "cook as you look" class while watching the video. This "learn as you go" technique works well for those who enjoy learning together.

Make a list of resource people and skills they can share.

_____

_____

_____

_____

_____

_____

_____

_____

_____

_____

_____

_____

_____

_____

_____

_____

_____

_____

_____

_____

_____

_____

CHAPTER 5

COMPLETING THE PREPAREDNESS PICTURE

It is our responsibility to provide for ourselves. We can learn to become self-reliant and independent by using wisely EVERYthing the Lord has given us, including our ability to learn to work hard. "We cannot be self-reliant without being willing to work. Work is physical, mental, or spiritual effort. The Lord has commanded us to work (See Genesis 3:17-19), for work is the source of happiness, self-esteem, and prosperity. It is the way we accomplish good things in our lives." (**Providing In The Lord's Way**, 1990, The Church of Jesus Christ of Latter-day Saints, Salt Lake City, UT.)

GETTING OUT OF DEBT
Learning to live on what we make and saving a little each month are two absolutely essential principles of a self-sufficient lifestyle. Make out a budget so you know approximately what you will receive and what you are going to spend. Then, learn ways to live on less. Do NOT spend what you do not have. Financial bondage should be avoided at all costs. Time and interest should be working FOR you, not against you.

According to the American Bar Association, over 90% of all divorces are related to money problems. Financial counselors indicate that only one out of five families is living on what it actually makes each month. In such prosperous economic times, how can this be? The problem lies not with a LACK of money, but how that money is managed. Wise counselors insist that debt should only be incurred for a home and possibly education. Learning self-discipline and self-restraint is essential where money is concerned, as well as in all other areas of life.

Young couples that expect to live in the same manner as they were accustomed to in their parents' homes fall prey to spending impulses and credit card debt. Genuine maturity is needed in our society that encourages self-indulgence and materialism. Buying on credit is easy. Paying back the debt and the interest that mounts daily is hard—sometimes impossible.

A friend told me that once they got behind on their payments, several companies actually RAISED their interest rates and made it impossible for them to refinance any of their loans anywhere else at a lower rate of interest. Over time, the interest actually grew to be larger than the original debt, and bankruptcy followed.

Making up a **Debt-Elimination Calendar** can help get you back on track faster than you ever thought possible. On a piece of paper, list the months of the year in a column on the left. Make additional columns for each creditor, starting with the one you want to pay off first. We chose the debt with the earliest pay-off date, but you might want to choose the one with the highest interest. List the monthly payment due under each creditor until the loan is repaid.

If you only owe five payments of $140 to Creditor A, list them across from the corresponding month in which you will make the payment. Do the same for Creditor B, C, D, and so on. (Hopefully, you won't need a larger sheet of paper!) If you were currently spending $530 on debts, divided among 4 creditors, you might have a chart that looked like this....

DEBT-ELIMINATION CALENDAR

	Credit Card 1	Credit Card 2	Auto Loan	Hospital
January	140	75	255	60
February	140	75	255	60
March	140	75	255	60
April	140	75	255	60
May	140	75	255	60
June		215	255	60
July		215	255	60
August			470	60
September			470	60
October			470	60
November				530
December				530

Once Credit Card 1 is paid off, the $140 is added to the bill for Credit Card 2, creating a new monthly payment of $215, then continuing the process until all loans are repaid.

A financial advisor has had fantastic success with helping people to get totally out of debt in only 8 years (including paying off their homes!!) by following the above program...with just a little extra commitment.

He asks first that each of his clients learn to manage their money better so they can add an extra $25 to the total amount they already pay each month. Second, any "extra" money that happens to come in (bonuses, gifts, etc.) is used to pay off debts. Third, vacations are restricted to local sites requiring as little cash as possible. Fourth, be realistic about what you think you need.

This may mean that the refrigerator you need to buy to replace the one that just died should be a USED one rather than a NEW one. Fifth, NO un-budgeted purchases (especially credit purchases) are to be made unless they are prayed about and an affirmative response is received.

The financial advisor teaching the class promised us that if we would make getting out of debt a firm commitment in our lives, the Lord would help us find ways to accomplish this in less than the customary 8 years. We decided to put this promise to the test. At the time, thanks to our use of the "Debt-Elimination Calendar," we were only in debt for our home, but we had very little equity in it.

Over the next 2 years, we were faced with buying 2 cars and moving across the country. By purchasing well-cared-for used cars; buying, storing and using only basic foods, combined with fresh fruits and vegetables; and spending as little as possible on moving and getting resettled, we will most likely achieve our goal within the next year... less than half the time we assumed it would take!   Provident living, working a little harder and a little longer each day, taking advantage of bargains and money-making opportunities, and honoring our commitment to stick to our budget has truly paid off!

LEARNING TO LIVE ON LESS

For many, learning to find creative ways to save money has proven to be a very rewarding and enjoyable challenge. One couple contracted with neighbors on their street to pick up the aluminum cans set out in the household recycling bins each week. The $100 a month they earned was saved for honeymoon expenses. A family of six saved hundreds of dollars each month by making their own mixes and preparing nutritious, meatless meals from beans and grains. One young mother learned how to use preventative measures to care for her family's health, saving the time spent in taking care of illnesses, trips to the doctor's office, and many hundreds of dollars each year in fees and prescriptions.

Many families buy almost exclusively from garage sales and second hand stores. A group of mothers near me engage in serious garage sale shopping. They often shop together, but they know what each other needs for their young children, so if one of them comes across one of those items, they'll buy it and pass it on.   I still have sewing supplies, but I stopped sewing for my family when I found I could buy "nearly new" high-quality clothing at garage sales and upscale thrift shops for far less than I would spend on the fabric alone. I never buy anything new when I can find it used and in excellent condition. I find satisfaction in knowing that I've "beat the system" by being able to fill my home with the things I need without being sucked into the black hole of debt.

BARTERING
There will be times when money is in short supply for one reason or another. What can you store that would be of value to someone else? What would you trade for? You may be able to trade one food for another, or allow someone to use your pressure cooker in exchange for their food dehydrator. You may want to make wheat jerky and trade for garden vegetables. If you're good at cooking up a nutritious meal of soup and bread, but are short on sprouting seeds or oil, you may be able to barter, or trade for those items.

Of course it is advisable to be totally self-sufficient, but most of us aren't totally prepared 100% of the time. We need to work together. In my family, we have allergies to wheat, but I still store a large amount and plan to use it to trade for something else of value. Plan to store extra of some things, especially basic foods (grains, legumes, and sprouting seeds), because they are compact, relatively inexpensive, and can easily sustain life.

You may have access to medical supplies, or gardening tools, or extra produce. Whatever you have on hand, store all you can and be prepared to barter. Many people barter skills - doctoring for dentistry, home repairs for tutoring, plumbing for carpentry, etc. Learning new skills and acquiring extra supplies will help ensure a more secure future.

CUTTING THE FOOD BILL
The amount spent on food, including eating out, is most often the easiest to cut. Switching from prepared foods and large quantities of meat to wholesome grains and beans, fresh fruits and vegetables saves money and improves health. The quality of whole foods prepared at home is far superior to "take out" in nutrient value and much less likely to contain artery-clogging fats and health-damaging preservatives and additives.

A typical monthly food budget of $450 for a family of four can easily be cut to $250 just by learning to cook with the basics. That's $1200 a year! That amount would go a long way toward getting out of debt and staying there.

SAVINGS

Pay yourself! Add a Savings Account column to your budget and save at least 5 percent of what you earn each month. If "learning to live on less" still isn't enough to leave you with 5% for savings, you may be able to find a part-time job that will provide the necessary funds. It is recommended that we each have at least three months' worth of savings to be used for essential family obligations if normal earnings were no longer available.

PHYSICAL HEALTH

What would you do for a doctor or medicines if you were without income for a year? Worse yet, what if all medical help and supplies were washed away by a flood, struck by lightning, blown away by a hurricane, lifted up and deposited who knows where by a tornado?

Learning to eat better, and to use preventive measures to heal the body rather than taking drugs to suppress symptoms is a very important part of a self-sufficient lifestyle. This can't be accomplished overnight. It takes months or trial and error, and even longer to change a lifetime of habits that are stressful to the body and the soul. Now is the time to begin, starting with the guidelines found in this book.

SPIRITUAL HEALTH

Developing an "attitude of gratitude," dwelling on the positive rather than the negative aspects of life is one of the best ways to build faith and hope for a brighter future. Those with hope always fare better when personal disasters come their way.

Learning to serve our Heavenly Father by serving others does more for our spiritual well-being than anything money can buy. When we help to lighten the burdens of others, Heavenly Father can make ours so light that they cannot even be felt. Gratitude, faith, hope and charity are the building blocks for a strong, healthy spirit.

JOB SKILLS

Getting the education you need to be able to work at a job you LIKE will enable you to support yourself and the ones you're responsible for. Are you happy with your job? Are you making enough money in your present profession, or do you need a better education and better skills? No one knows when the family wage earner(s) will be without work. Everyone should develop skills (and keep them current) in an alternate field that will pay more than minimum wage and help you avoid prolonged unemployment.

BECOME A "HANDYMAN"

With the abundance of How-To books in libraries and stores to help us get started, there's no reason why we can't learn what we need to know in order to make minor home repairs, and perform car maintenance. In my family, there are times when we choose to hire someone to help because it helps out the person doing the job and costs less than taking time away from our regular jobs to do it ourselves. The most important part of being prepared is knowing HOW to do things on your own. Whether or not you NEED to do them on a regular basis doesn't matter. At least you are prepared to do them, should the need arise.

CHILDREN NEED TO LEARN THE IMPORTANCE OF WORK

Involve family members in maintenance and repair projects. "In the sweat of thy brow shalt thou eat bread" is basic to personal preparedness. Parents who allow children to grow up gathering their "green stuff" from the family money tree aren't doing them any favors! Helping family members to learn to work for what they earn and save for what they need will enable them to spend wisely, and make responsible financial decisions.

PUTTING YOUR DOCUMENTS IN ORDER

Most natural disasters can be tracked and advance efforts are made to evacuate, giving people time to gather their important documents and information. In my area of the country, "tornado alley," whole houses can disappear in a matter of seconds. Each year as I see disastrous events all around me, I see the wisdom in having a 2nd set of records such as birth certificates, wills, and other legal documents, financial information, medical records, genealogy and family history.

With severe weather and other natural disasters on the rise, it makes sense to have important documents in several parts of the country. Our daughter-in-law laminated 2 extra copies of all their important papers and mailed them to both sets of parents.

Don't wait for an emergency. Use this **Passport To Survival** to help you make a plan and follow it — one step at a time, BEFORE disaster strikes.

Appendix 1
Cooking Measurements and Substitutions

T.	=	tablespoon	qt.	=	quart
t.	=	teaspoon	4 c.	=	quart
3 t.	=	1 T.	gal.	=	gallon
4 T.	=	1/4 cup	4 qt.	=	1 gallon
c.	=	cup	16 c.	=	1 gallon

WHEAT
- 2 1/2 cups of wheat = 1 pound.
- It takes 1 1/2 cups of wheat (9 oz.) to make 2 1/2 cups of flour.
- 1 cup of wheat will make 1 quart of wheat sprouts.

BEANS
- 2 cups of beans equals 1 pound.
- 1 cup of most beans will make 3-4 cups of bean sprouts.

BATTER AND DOUGH
- 1 measure of flour to 1 measure of liquid makes a pourable batter.
- 2 measure of flour to 1 measure of liquid makes a drop batter.
- 3 measures of flour to 1 measure of liquid makes a soft dough.
- 4 measures of flour to 1 measure of liquid makes a stiff dough.

SALT
- Use 1 t. salt to 3 cups of liquid for cereals, soups and gravies.
- In breadmaking, use 1/2 t. salt to every cup of flour.

MILK
- Use 3 T. dry milk powder (non-instant) to 1 cup water.
- Use 3/4 c. dry milk powder (non-instant) to 1 quart water.
- Use 1 1/3 c. instant (crystals) milk to 1 quart water.

Substitutions
If you don't have eggs on hand, or want to stay away from cholesterol, try these options to replace 1 egg:
- 1 t. baking powder
  1 T. water
  1 T. vinegar

- 1 pkg. plain gelatin
  2 T. warm water
  (Add gelatin to dry ingredients, water to moist ingredients.)

- 1 t. yeast in 1/4 c. warm water

- 1 T. apricot pureé

- 1 1/2 T. water
  1 T. olive oil
  1 t. baking powder

Appendix 2
Words Of Warning and Of Wisdom
From Modern-Day Prophets

Since 1937, the prophets of the Church of Jesus Christ of Latter-day Saints have urged their members to be more self-sufficient, to rely less on what can be bought from the store and more on what can be produced at home. This need for this counsel is becoming increasingly more obvious as we witness almost daily natural and man-made disasters; as the world economy grows more unstable; and as personal bankruptcies continue to rise at an overwhelmingly alarming rate. We would do well to follow these words of wisdom...

"Maintain a year's supply. The Lord has urged that his people save for the rainy days, prepare for the difficult times, and put away for emergencies, a year's supply or more of bare necessities so that when comes the flood, the earthquake, the famine, the hurricane, the storms of life, our families can be sustained through the dark days." (Teachings of Spencer W. Kimball, p. 374)

"When distress or disaster comes to any of our people, we must be ready to help each other. As we become more affluent and our bank accounts enlarge, there comes a feeling of security, and we feel sometimes that we do not need the supply that has been suggested by the Brethren. It lies there and deteriorates, we say (and it DOES if we do not learn to use it). And suppose it does? We can re-establish it. We must remember that conditions could change and a year's supply of basic commodities could be very much appreciated by us or others. So we would do well to listen to what we have been told and to follow it explicitly." (Teachings of Spencer W. Kimball, p. 375)

"Plant gardens. Follow the counsel to have gardens wherever possible so that we do not lose contact with the soil and so that we can have the security of being able to provide at least some of our food and necessities. Grow vegetables and eat those grown in your own yard. Even those residing in apartments or condominiums can generally grow a little food in pots and planters. Gardens promote independence. Should the trucks fail to fill the shelves of the stores, many would go hungry. How do we evaluate the good that comes from the obvious lessons of planting, cultivating, and the eternal law of the harvest? And how do we measure the family togetherness and cooperating that must accompany successful canning? Yes, we are laying up resources in store, but perhaps the greater good is contained in the lessons of life we learn as we live providently and extend to our children their pioneer heritage." (Teachings of Spencer W. Kimball, p. 376)

Ezra Taft Benson, in 1974, challenged us to be self-sustaining through adequate preparation. "An almost forgotten means of economic self-reliance is the home production of food. We are too accustomed to going to stores and purchasing what we need. By producing some of our food we reduce, to a great extent, the impact of inflation on our money." (Teachings of Ezra Taft Benson, p. 265-266)

He spoke of the blessings of growing a garden, even a small one, to raise our own food. He said "Noah built his ark BEFORE the flood came, and he and his family survived. Those who waited to act until after the flood began were too late." He warned "The days ahead are sobering and challenging. ...Let us not be dissuaded from preparing because of a seeming prosperity today, or a so-called peace." He also said "The revelation to store food may be as essential to our temporal salvation today as boarding the ark was to the people in the days of Noah." (The Ensign, January, 1974.)

"We know that the Lord has decreed global calamities for the future and has warned and forewarned us to be prepared. For this reason, the Brethren have repeatedly stressed a "back to basics" program for temporal and spiritual welfare." (Teachings of Ezra Taft Benson, p. 267)

"The Saints have been advised to pay their own way and maintain a cash reserve. Recent history has demonstrated that in difficult days it is reserves with intrinsic value that are of most worth, rather than reserves the value of which may be destroyed through inflation. It is well to remember that continued government deficits cause inflation; inflation is used as an excuse for ineffective price controls, price controls lead to shortages; artificial shortages inevitably are used as an excuse to implement rationing. When will we learn these basic economic principles?" (**Teachings of Ezra Taft Benson**, p. 267)

Gordon B. Hinckley, on Oct. 3, 1998 counseled us "to get our houses in order." He stressed that we cannot be self-reliant when we are in debt for more than a modest house. We have neither freedom nor independence when we have debt hanging over us. Even Benjamin Franklin recognized the dangers of financial bondage. "Think what you do when you run in debt, ...you give to another power over your liberty."

Orson Hyde, over 125 years ago, said "...Store up all your grain, and take care of it!...And I tell you it is almost as necessary to have bread to sustain the body as it is to have food for the spirit; for the one is as necessary as the other to enable us to carry on the work of God upon the earth." (**Journal of Discourses**, vol. 5, p. 17.)

****

The following articles on Home Storage have appeared in the *Ensign*, published by the Church of Jesus Christ of Latter-day Saints:

Home Storage: Build On The Basics, June 1989, p. 39.	Giving New Life To Old Beans, Jan. 1990, p. 74	Sprouting Up, Mar. 1994, p. 72
Tracking Our Food Storage, Feb. 1996, p. 71	Heaps More - With Wheat, Aug. 1991, p. 71	Plastic Bag It!, Mar. 1995, p. 71
Home Storage- How To Begin, April 1986, p. 64	Mmmmm! This Couldn't Be Food Storage, Mar. 1990, p. 71	Taking The Bite Out Of Food Storage, Mar. 1992, p. 72
Whole Wheat - In Disguise, Aug. 1990, p. 71	Spice Up Your Rice, Feb. 1990, p. 73	If Ye Are Prepared Ye Shall Not Fear, Nov. 1995, p. 35
Discovering Lentils, June 1994, p. 71	Using That Powdered Milk, Mar. 1991, p. 72	Preparation = Peace, Sept. 1992, p. 61
Barley Surviving, Jan. 1992, p 72	Frugal Food Storage, Jan. 1993, p. 73	When the Lights Go Out, June, 1992, p. 71
Do You Know Beans About Beans? June 1991, p. 66	Getting Into The (Wheat) Grind, Jan. 1991, p. 72	Beyond Band-aids, Mar. 1992, p. 73

Appendix 3
Most Often-Asked Questions about Storage Foods

Q. What do I look for in buying a mill to grind grains and beans?
A. 1) A good guarantee, in writing! Any mill will grind grains, but some manufacturers say they will not guarantee their mill will grind beans. Any mill is bound to malfunction at one time or another, but some companies stand behind their products and others make excuses why you should be responsible for payment on expensive repairs. I have had the best customer service with the K-TEC Kitchen Mill. 2) Look for one that mills at low temperatures to best preserve nutrients.

Q. What is the shelf life of bean and grain flours?
A. Beans and grains have a protective, full-of-fiber outer shell. Once that is broken, nutrients decrease and deterioration begins. Fresh flours should be used within 1-2 weeks or refrigerated. (Zip-loc freezer bags and wide mouth quart jars filled with bean flours freeze well and are easy to use.) Ideally, flours should be ground just before using, but that is not always possible. I have kept bean flours on the shelf for more than a year as a test. While no flavor change can usually be detected, I know that nutrients have been lost.

Q. I don't have time to cook brown rice and whole or cracked wheat before I even start preparing a meal, so I always end up using instant white rice. Help!
A. Cooked grains and beans can be frozen in 2-cup portions in quart zip-loc freezer bags for up to 6 months. I fill the bags, then flatten and press out as much air as possible. After zipping shut, I lay them flat in the freezer on a baking tray. When frozen, I stack them 6-8 high on one side of my freezer. To thaw, place the bag in a pan of warm water or defrost in the microwave.

Q. Do I have to wash beans before grinding? I wash them before cooking, why not before grinding?
A. Years ago, packages of dry beans from the grocery store and especially from food storage sources, used to contain rocks, small dirt clods and

dust. Nowdays, beans are usually "triple cleaned." While you may find an occasional chunk of dirt, the beans themselves are usually shiny and clean. I pour 2 cups of beans at a time into the hopper of my mill and sort them as they are being ground.

Q. How can I add fiber to fast foods? Most of the time, that's all my family will eat! Usually, they only want what comes from a can or a box!
A. Sneak it in! Find some of their favorite foods (pizza, tacos, hamburgers) and fortify them by adding bean flours, cooked beans and grains. If you have a take-out pizza, sprinkle the top with a cup of cooked brown rice and cover it up with extra olives and cheese. If you use ground beef or ground poultry to make tacos or burgers, add 1/4 cup of bean flour and 1 cup of cooked brown rice to each cup of ground meat. Season with 2-3 t. beef or chicken bouillon or a packaged seasoning mix.

Q. How do I keep my family from dictating what foods I prepare?
A. Nutrition is serious business, and we have a stewardship to take the best care possible of the bodies we've been given. Parents have the responsibility to teach and train children to enjoy nutritious foods. Try having a family council and letting everyone help decide the menu for one high-fiber, super nutritious meal each week. Vary the menu and you'll come up with a good variety of family favorites. After a few months, add another "nutrition day." Gradually sneak in beans, bean flours and grains to their traditional favorites. Most people can't even tell the difference, except they are more quickly satisfied and stay full longer! That's a real plus when you're feeding teenagers!

Q. I tossed out all my prepared foods and started feeding my family whole wheat bread and whole-grain cereals and veggie burgers instead of hamburgers. Now they all have diarrhea and I'm in the doghouse. What can I do?
A. "Buck Up" and get used to it? No, this is a REAL problem and occurs when meals are not balanced with proper amounts of vegetables and beans. Gradually increasing the amount of whole grains is safest.

Q. Why are wheat, beans and rice considered "basic" foods?
A. Grains and legumes combine to form a complete protein. Soybeans are complete by themselves. Vegetable proteins are more readily digestible and easier for our bodies to utilize.

Q. Why are cracked grains and beans used?
A. Cracking, like cutting or grating large vegetables, speeds cooking time. See COUNTRY BEANS, for more fast ways to use bean flour, which is milled from dry beans and cooks in only 3 minutes for fast fat-free soups, sauces, gravies, and much more.

Q. Why are cracked grains, beans and wheat flour refrigerated?
A. As soon as the hard outer shell of dried grains and legumes is broken or removed, nutrients begin to deteriorate and go rancid. Freezing stops this action.

Q. Why is it so important to add grains and beans to almost every recipe?
A. The Benson Institute (Brigham Young University, Provo, Utah 84602) research supports the USDA findings and indicates that 50-60% of calories should come from grain and grain products and legumes (beans). Most of those grains and beans should be WHOLE grains, meaning whole, cracked, or ground into flour, but not processed. Dividing your year's supply into daily portions, 300 lb. of grains would average 5+ cups of cooked or sprouted grains daily! Using and storing a variety of grains and legumes is ESSENTIAL!

Q. What if I am allergic to wheat?
A. Thousands of people have been diagnosed with an allergy to wheat. This poses a definite problem, but there IS an answer! All recipes calling for whole or cracked wheat, and many breads using baking powder or soda as a leavening agent, can be altered to use rice flour or other grain flours in place of wheat flour. Health food stores usually carry alternative gluten-free flours. A recipe is included in Country Beans to make your own gluten-free mix at home.

Q. Why aren't meat recipes included?
A. Although I am not a vegetarian and use meat occasionally, research shows that meat is not NECESSARY to obtain complete protein with proper combining of grains and vegetables and legumes. Most meats are kept frozen, a luxury we may not have in the event of widespread electrical failure.

Q. What are some good sources of protein?
A. The Benson Institute suggests that 10 to 20% of our calories should come from protein foods and the easiest to store are fortified dry milk, tuna fish, and beans (legumes).

Q. What kind of fats should I use?
A. Vegetable oil (olive oil is best), and peanut butter can be stored to provide the necessary 5-10% of our calories that should come from fats, according to the Benson Institute. The American diet typically consists of more than 40% fat, far more than is necessary.

Q. In desserts, crackers, pancakes, etc., that call for wheat flour, why mix ingredients ONLY until moistened?
A. Because the gluten in wheat flour is quickly developed and dough becomes tough. Very few recipes call for beating.

Q. When baking, why are honey recipes more brown?
A. Honey darkens when heated and tends to burn easily in some recipes.

Sprout Questions and Answers

Q. How many sprouts do we have to eat to get a full day's supply of vitamin C?
A. The general rule of thumb is 1/2 cup. Sprouts with leaves allowed to turn green are the highest in ALL nutrients.

Q. How do I keep sprouts from going sour or slimy?
A. Rinsing 2-3 times a day, with PROPER DRAINAGE after each rinsing will keep sprouts fresh.

Q. My husband and family say they won't eat sprouts. How can I sneak them in so they won't notice?
A. Sprouted beans look much the same as regular beans, so try soups, chili, as well as chopped sprouts in patties. If necessary, break off the sprout tails and blend them with other liquid ingredients.

Q. How long do sprouts keep in the refrigerator?
A. For optimum nutrition, sprouts store only 3-4 days, but some varieties will actually keep up to 2 weeks.

Q. Why do mung and soy sprouts turn green when I try to sprout them long?
A. The presence of light causes greening, so make sure they are kept completely in the dark.

Q. Can the "gas" from beans be eliminated?
A. Pinto and kidney beans are the most likely to cause gas. Sprouting adds enzymes that change indigestible carbohydrates to digestible carbohydrates. Even though cooking would destroy those enzymes, the carbohydrates would still be in a more usable form. Beans cooked at low temperatures would be best. Tolerance for high fiber foods, like beans and whole grains, increases when those foods are eaten often.

Cheese Questions and Answers

Q. Can cheese be stored?
A. Yes, it can be frozen or wrapped in vinegar soaked cloth or paraffin and stored in a cool place. Several varieties can easily be made from powdered milk. Most cheeses can be made in only 3 minutes!!) using newly developed techniques.

Q. What acids can be used to curdle milk?
A. Any acid will curdle milk. The best tasting cheeses are made with rennet, fresh lemon juice, reconstituted lemon juice, white vinegar and ascorbic acid.

Q. If cheeses are just made with dry milk, water and an acid, will they taste good by themselves?
A. You can add buttermilk, salt and other flavorings (see below), but I most often use the dry cheese curds in salads, sandwich fillings, patties and casseroles. They are meant to add protein, not to add flavor.

Q. What seasonings can I use to flavor homemade cheeses?
A. Salt, onion and garlic salt, seasoned salts, parsley, chives, sesame seeds, caraway seeds, green chilies, hot peppers, olives, pimiento and buttermilk. If you mix these cheeses with commercial cheese and use in a recipe, most people will never be able to tell the difference.

Q. What if I only have instant milk? Can I use this in your recipes?
A. Instant crystals (the grocery store variety) are fluffier than powdered, but they can be blended to a powder, then used in any of my recipes. When making milk, 3 cups of the non-instant powdered milk I use makes 1 gallon of liquid milk.

Appendix 4
Glossary

Bran, Flaked - The outer hull of the whole grain (wheat or oats) which is removed in the process of making white flour. A great source of fiber.

Brown Rice - Unlike most whole grains with the bran and germ intact, brown rice will go rancid within 2-4 months unless refrigerated or frozen. There are over a thousand different varieties of cultivated rice, so experiment with the ones available to you to find your favorites. Basmati brown rice is our all-time family favorite, even for those who thought they only loved white rice.

Bulgur - Whole wheat that has been boiled, dried, and sometimes cracked. Cooks in the same amount of time as raw cracked wheat.

Buckwheat - Generally used in the flour form in specialty pancake mixes. Sprouted buckwheat makes a delicious lettuce substitute.

Canola Oil - A readily available vegetable made from rapeseed. It contains the lowest amounts of saturated fat. Recent research indicates that this oil, probably because of the refining process, may actually be harmful. Virgin olive oil, is still best.

Carob - A healthy alternative to chocolate that does NOT contain caffeine. It can be found in powdered or bar form at health stores, candy shops and some grocery stores.

Cracked Wheat - Wheat cracked at home cooks in only 15 minutes. It often contains very fine particles and flour that need to be sifted out and used as cereal or in baking.

Farina - The fine particles sifted out of wheat that is cracked at home. Makes a cereal like Cream of Wheat.

Gluten - The isolated protein part of wheat. After wheat is ground into flour, the gluten can be separated from the other components by a stirring and rinsing process. The resulting gluten is a stretchy, elastic-like product that is insoluble in water and can take on various textures when prepared with certain techniques.

Hulled White Sesame Seeds - More readily available than brown sesame seeds, and are preferred when making sesame "milk" for use in breakfast shakes. Toasted seeds are excellent over Chinese dishes and salads.

Soybeans - The only legume that contains all 8 essential amino acids for a complete protein. Also high in calcium. Used as a coarsely cracked grain (grits), as a flour, soymilk and tofu.

Soy Sauce - Fermented soybean juice. Tamari sauce is the only variety without MSG and preservatives. Great for seasoning gravies, casseroles, rice, and millet.

Sucanat® - Evaporated cane juice, granulated; contains all the vitamins and minerals of cane juice. Manufactured by NutraCane, Inc., 5 Meadowbrook Parkway, Milford, NH 03055.

Sunflower Seeds - Whole seeds, raw or toasted, seasoned or plain, make a great high protein snack. Ground seeds make a meal that can be added to breads, cereals and nut-butters. Sprouted sunflower seeds make an excellent lettuce replacement in salads or sandwiches.

Tofu - The curd from soy milk, made like cheese curd from cow's milk. Bland-tasting, but very versatile. It can be sliced, cubed or blended and used in place of meat and cheese...without the saturated fat and cholesterol from dairy products.

Vegetable Broth and Bouillon- Even though I have several favorite meat-based bouillons, I prefer SOUPerior Bean's vegetarian broths. They come in chicken, beef, and vegetable flavors. All are meat-free. To order, call 1-800-878-7687, or contact Duane Rough at the company's headquarters, P. O. Box 753, Brush Prairie, WA 98606.

Yeast - Recently, instant yeast has become popular, but most recipes calling for whole grain flours turn out better using regular active dry yeast. These flours contain more "heavy" bran and fiber than refined flours and take longer to rise successfully.

Appendix 5
Grocery Shopping List

As consumers demand them, more and more grocery stores are beginning to carry wholesome foods. Check out the shelves of your grocery or health food store, or your local co-op and try some of these favorites from my shopping list. Most fall into the "extras" category, but we splurge as often as the budget will allow.

Nutritional Supplements
- acidophilus powder
- aloe vera juice
- brewer's yeast
- C-Crystals (vitamin C powder)
- flaxseed oil-Barlean's
- Juice Plus+
- liquid chlorophyll
- spirulina or barley green

Flavorings - Sweeteners
- carob powder
- honey
- malted milk powder
- pure maple syrup
- flavored extracts (vanilla, etc.)

Fruits - fresh/frozen/dried
- apples
- applesauce, unsweetened
- apricots
- avocado
- bananas
- blackberries
- blueberries
- cantaloupe
- casaba melon
- honeydew melon
- kiwi fruit
- lemon
- lime
- mango
- pineapple
- pineapple chunks, canned in juice
- pineapple, crushed, canned in juice
- oranges
- papayas
- peaches
- pears

- plums
- red grapes
- raisins
- raspberries
- red apples
- strawberries
- watermelon

100% Fruit Juices
- Black Cherry Juice-Knudsen
- Apricot Nectar-Knudsen
- cranberry juice
- fruit punch
- fresh-squeezed grapefruit juice
- lemon juice- bottled
- Vita Juice-Simply Nutritious
- Pineapple Juice-Del Monte
- papaya nectar

100% Fruit Juice Concentrates
- orange juice
- apple juice
- grape juice
- creamed papaya

Dole 100% Fruit Juice Concentrates
- Country Raspberry
- Mountain Cherry
- Pineapple Orange
- Pineapple-Orange Banana
- Pineapple-Orange Strawberry
- Pineapple Juice

Welch's 100% Fruit Juice Concentrates
- White Grape
- White Grape Cranberry
- White Grape Peach
- White Grape Raspberry

Whole Grains or Grain Flours
- ❏ amaranth
- ❏ barley
- ❏ buckwheat
- ❏ corn
- ❏ millet
- ❏ oats
- ❏ quinoa
- ❏ rice-brown
- ❏ rye
- ❏ spelt
- ❏ triticale
- ❏ wheat

Legumes
- ❏ anasazi beans
- ❏ adzuki beans
- ❏ black beans
- ❏ blackeyed peas
- ❏ garbanzo beans
- ❏ Great Northern beans
- ❏ green lentils
- ❏ green peas
- ❏ kidney beans
- ❏ lima beans
- ❏ mung beans
- ❏ navy beans
- ❏ peanuts
- ❏ pink beans
- ❏ pinto beans
- ❏ red beans
- ❏ red lentils
- ❏ small white beans
- ❏ soy beans
- ❏ tofu & soy products
- ❏ yellow peas

Milk - Dry
- ❏ non-fat powdered milk- non-instant
- ❏ buttermilk powder

Milks - Non-Dairy (liquid or powder)
(or make your own!)
- ❏ almond milk-Pacific Foods
- ❏ oat milk
- ❏ soy beverage, non fat-WestSoy
- ❏ rice milk, fat free, plain
- ❏ soy milk, regular, lite or fat-free

Nuts, Seeds
- ❏ alfalfa seeds
- ❏ almonds
- ❏ broccoli seeds
- ❏ cabbage seeds
- ❏ cashews
- ❏ clover seeds
- ❏ filberts
- ❏ flax seeds
- ❏ pecans
- ❏ pine nuts
- ❏ poppy seeds
- ❏ pumpkin seeds
- ❏ radish seeds
- ❏ brown sesame seeds
- ❏ sunflower seeds
- ❏ walnuts

Nut/Seed Butters
- ❏ almond butter
- ❏ sesame seeds, unhulled
- ❏ tahini (sesame butter)

Bouillons
- ❏ Better Than Bouillon®- Superior Touch Vegetarian Vegetable
- ❏ HerbOx bouillons - without MSG

Tofu
- ❏ any brand - choose from low-fat or regular

Vegetables
- ❏ asparagus
- ❏ beans, green
- ❏ beets and greens
- ❏ cabbage family
- ❏ carrots
- ❏ ginger root
- ❏ kohlrabi
- ❏ mushrooms
- ❏ parsley
- ❏ potatoes, all types
- ❏ red and green bell peppers
- ❏ spinach
- ❏ squash, all types
- ❏ Swiss chard
- ❏ tomatoes

INDEX

PUBLICATIONS WORTH ORDERING

Natural Meals Publishing • 1-888-232-6706
www.naturalmeals.com
E-mail - info@naturalmeals.com • sales@naturalmeals.com

COUNTRY BEANS *by Rita Bingham*
Learn to cook beans in only 3 minutes! Nearly 400 quick, easy meatless bean recipes with over 110 bean flour recipes, including FAST, fat-free 3-minute bean soups and 5-minute bean dips. Learn how to grind your own bean, pea and lentil flours, or where to purchase them. Most recipes are wheat-free, gluten-free, dairy-free. Recipes for every meal. *Guaranteed* to change the way you use beans! **$14.95**

NATURAL MEALS IN MINUTES *by Rita Bingham*
Learn to cook grains in only 15 minutes! Over 300 quick, high-fiber, low-fat, meatless recipes using basic storage foods. Learn sneaky tricks on adding extra fiber to every meal. Reduce the risk of heart attack and other diseases.
• FAST meals using Grains and Beans
• Bean, Seed and Grain Sprouts
• 3-minute fat-free Powdered Milk Cheeses.
Guaranteed to please! Each recipe lists nutritional data. **$14.95**

1-2-3 SMOOTHIES *by Rita Bingham*

123 Quick Frosty Drinks - Delicious AND Nutritious! Is there one perfect breakfast—afternoon snack— meal-on-the-run—or one perfect way to sneak nutritious vitamins and other important nutrients into a finicky eater? YES! It's a 1-2-3 Smoothie! These energy-boosting, nutritious drinks are the hottest COOL healthy treats ever! 100% natural ingredients - no sugar, preservatives, artificial sweeteners, or added fat. **$14.95**

Quick **WHOLESOME FOODS** video with *free* recipe booklet *by Bingham and Moulton*

Whether you're preparing for emergencies, or just want to make quick, inexpensive meals, you'll learn to make fantastically easy recipes like:
- Light, fluffy, 100% whole wheat breads
- Meatless spicy sausage, and thick steaklets
- Non-fat 3-minute powdered milk cheeses
- 3-minute bean soups and cream sauces

Make delicious, nutritious, vegetarian meals from stored foods in 30 minutes or less. 65 minutes, VHS **$29.95**

FOOD COMBINING Better Health—The *Natural* Way *by Rita Bingham*

Take CHARGE of your health! Learn to use and combine the best foods on earth...*Fruits, Vegetables, Grains, Legumes, Nuts and Seeds.*
- Experience vibrant health
- Find and maintain your proper weight
- Learn how to prevent and even reverse illnesses such as cancer, heart disease, arthritis, and more!
- Complete protein meals—without animal products

80 pages. **$6.95**

SAUCES, SEASONINGS AND NATURAL MEALS *by Rita Bingham*

Over 200 recipes using whole foods to create healthy sauces, seasonings, and delicious, nutritious meals — from home-style to gourmet! Meals ready in a FLASH and guaranteed to please! Most recipes are gluten-free, dairy-free,with no added fats, sugar or preservatives.

Salads and Dressings • Spice Blends
Seasoning Mixes • Quick Mixes • Fruit Sauces
Pasta Sauces • Marinades • Dips • Spreads
Fat-Free Gravies and MUCH more!

$15.95   *Available February, 2000*

Please add $3.50 shipping for 1st item, 50¢ for each additional item.

Dealers, call for pricing and terms.

Update on the *original* Passport To Survival author, Esther Dickey

Esther at 83—Busy As A Bee

When Esther Dickey wrote Passport To Survival in 1967, she was 52 years old. What a strange coincidence that I, her next to the youngest daughter, am the very same age as I revise and republish her book, 32 years later.

Esther's father was a beekeeper and one has to be a real "worker bee" to keep up with her!!!! Like the honey bee, she is industrious. She is the most prepared person I know. Her most favorite motto is "Use it up, wear it out, make it do, or do without!" She is magnificent at making something out of nothing. Growing up in the Depression years, she lived with very few material possessions. This taught her to find a use for everything and to waste nothing.

In the last 30 years, Esther has traveled around the world twice, giving lectures and demonstrations, and learning survival skills to share with others. She has always practiced what she preaches, constantly experimenting with new recipes, the latest gardening techniques, emergency clothing for hot or cold weather, and new survival equipment.

Until recently she had surplus "stuff" for every possibly emergency stored in multiple pantries, basements, attics, garages, and barns. She has supplied more families with food, clothing, furniture and even craft supplies than any of her 5 living children could possibly count. When we convinced her to simplify her life and slow down a little, she sorted, cleaned and discarded with her traditional "busy bee" enthusiasm....and in record time! She now shares inspiring messages instead of "stuff."

She still grows and harvests nearly all of her own food. It is hard for her to drive (something she still does *only* with the help of guardian angels!) past the fields near her home without stopping to glean excess beets, cabbage, carrots and greens after the harvests are over.

She still keeps mentally active. Last year, she made a video of her life, bought a new computer, learned "Windows 95," and figured out how to use e-mail. This year, she bought a scanner and will learn to use it to put photographs into our family newsletters.

As of yet, she hasn't parachuted from an airplane, but if invited, she'd relish the opportunity to be the oldest Great Great Grandmother to learn. What a woman! Thanks, Mom!